CONTENTS

ACKNOWLEDGMENTS

The completion of this undertaking could not have been possible without the participation and support of so many people whose names may not all be enumerated. Their contributions are sincerely appreciated and gratefully acknowledged. However, I would like to express my deep appreciation and indebtedness particularly to the following people:

- My mentor Rafael Riqueni, who taught me so deeply in a personal and professional level.
- Peter Alhadeff, one of the great teachers I had at Berklee College of Music, who encouraged me towards the completion of this task.
- Jonathan Feist, who always trusted in my work.
- My colleagues Jose Ignacio Cordobés Fernández, Abraham Padilla, Piti Martínez, and Sergio Martínez.
- To my sponsors Conde Hermanos, Jesús de Jiménez, and Knobloch Strings.
- Thanks to AIE for trusting in my work and supporting me during my masters program at Berklee College of Music.
- To all my relatives, friends, and others that in one way or another shared their support, both morally and physically.

To all of you, thank you so much.
—Yago Santos

PREFACE

This book and its accompanying audio and video provide guitarists with the fundamental techniques for playing flamenco guitar, as well as a detailed description of the peculiarities that make this instrument and style of music unique.

It is designed for guitarists with basic technique and reading ability, and requires no prior knowledge of flamenco music. It will help you to play in the flamenco style, and also to add elements of flamenco to whatever style of music you play.

This study begins with an explanation of the flamenco guitar as an instrument, its construction and performance possibilities, and its roles throughout history.

In the first part, "Theory and Concepts," you will learn and practice the rhythmic cycles employed in flamenco music, as well as the main chords, scales, and cadences. In this section, we will also get deep into flamenco form by understanding the *palo* and *falseta* and how to properly identify, create, and classify them.

In part II, "Flamenco Guitar Techniques," the techniques employed in flamenco guitar will be explained and illustrated with exercises and demonstration tracks for each concept, supported with audio and video that you can access online. See the first page of this book for the URL and your unique access code for this material.

Finally, the book contains twenty-four original falsetas, also with audio and video, which you can play over seven palos (soleá, fandangos de Huelva, guajira... see lesson 4) with percussion tracks recorded by Sergio Martínez.

In the appendixes, you will find a list of recommended listening with recordings that made a significant contribution to this music, an introduction to alternative tunings, and a glossary of common Spanish guitar terms.

ABOUT THE AUDIO AND VIDEO

To access the accompanying audio and video that support the following lessons, go to www.halleonard.com/mylibrary and enter the code found on the first page of this book. This will grant you instant access to every example. Examples with accompanying media are marked with the following icons:

INTRODUCTION TO FLAMENCO GUITAR

FEATURES OF FLAMENCO GUITAR

There are three major aspects that make flamenco guitar different from any other guitar type: the instrument itself, the way it is played, and its sound. These unique qualities are strongly related to the accompaniment role that the guitar has played in traditional flamenco music, as well as to the ingenuity of the early flamenco guitarists. The repertoire, concepts, and techniques were orally transmitted. Despite the absence of a formal music education system for writing about the music and training flamenco musicians, they created the unique musical system, set of techniques, and sounds that are broadly recognized as flamenco.

The first flamenco-style guitar was built in the mid-nineteenth century in southern Spain by the legendary Spanish guitar maker (*guitarrero*) Antonio de Torres (Almería, 1817 to 1892).

Besides building the first flamenco guitar, this mid-nineteenth century craftsman also redesigned the modern Spanish classical guitar, giving it its definitive form. He increased the size of the body; set the proportions between the upper bout, the waist, and the lower bout; and introduced the seven-brace system and the mechanical tuning peg (among other things). All these improvements gave the guitar a new range of power, volume, dynamics, color, and expression, and it thus became a more viable concert instrument.

The first flamenco guitars built by Torres in the 1860s reveal that, in comparison with Spanish classical guitars, their construction is characterized by a smaller body, the use of Spanish cypress for the back and the sides, a five-brace system instead of the seven used in classical guitars, a lower bridge and saddle (which facilitates the movement of the fretting hand *ligados* and *picados*), and the tapping plate (*golpeador*) to protect the top of the guitar.

These significant elements, which are not necessarily visible, made this guitar meet the requirements of flamenco music (higher volume, more brilliant and percussive sound suitable for the voice and dance accompaniment), and the budget range of the early flamenco guitarists (use of cheaper woods and simpler construction).

PARTS OF A FLAMENCO GUITAR

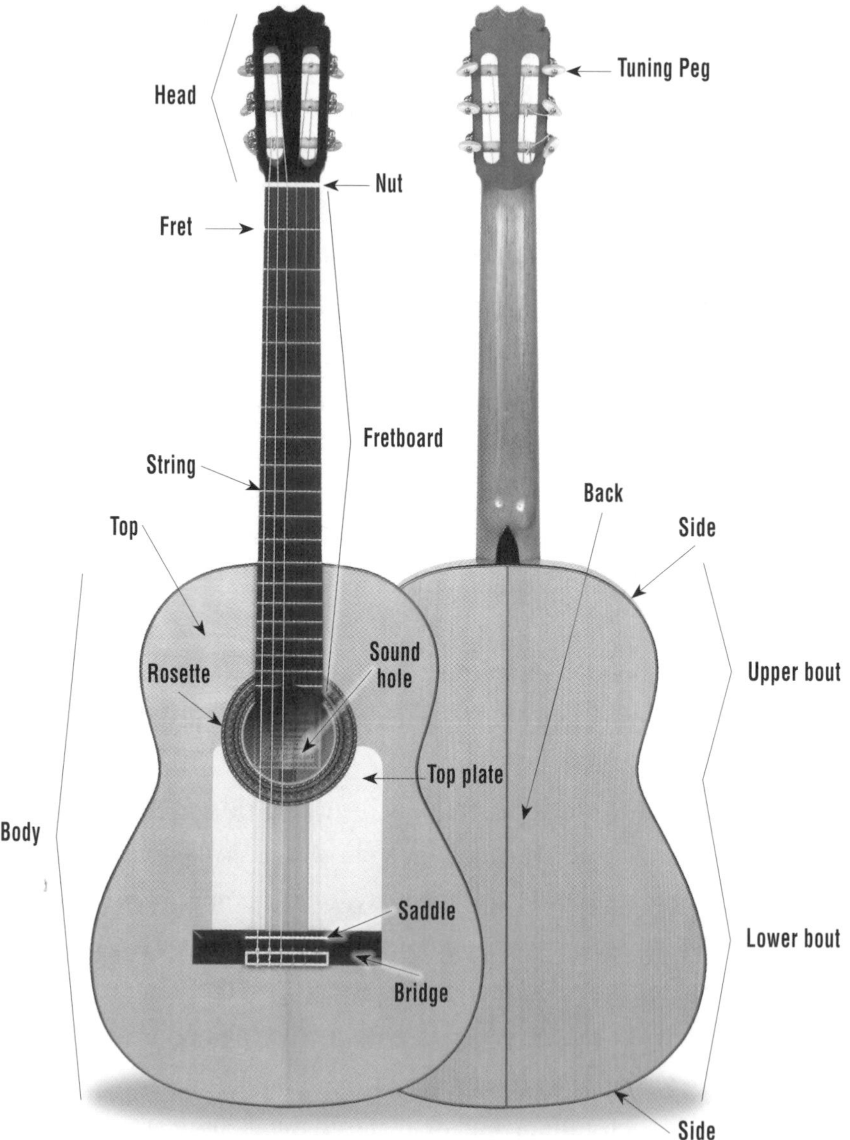

FIG. I.1. Parts of a Flamenco Guitar

CLASSICAL GUITAR VS. FLAMENCO GUITAR

When playing flamenco, you can use either a classical or a flamenco guitar. However, a classical guitar won't be optimized for the percussive and rhythmic effects that characterize flamenco.

Both classical and flamenco guitars share the same shape, similar size, head, number of frets, strings, and tuning (E, A, D, G, B, E); that is why they look so similar at first glance. However, the instruments differ in four major ways: in the way they are built, in the materials used to build them, in the action and playability of the strings, and in the sound/tones they produce.

The body and neck of the flamenco guitar are slightly thinner and narrower than the types used on a classical guitar. The strings are also closer to the soundboard and fingerboard (lower action), which facilitates the fast fretting-hand *ligados* and *picados*, as well as the strumming-hand *rajeos* (or *rasgueados*) and tapping or percussion (*golpe*) on the guitar itself. The lower bridge setup of the flamenco guitar also makes the response faster and the tone brighter and punchier. In addition, as the strings are closer to the frets, there is a greater chance of buzzing (*chasqueo*). This is not an issue for flamenco players; indeed, it is considered part of the percussive character of the flamenco guitar sound.

On the other hand, classical guitars are built with a slightly wider and thicker body and neck, and higher action at the bridge, nut, and saddle. This allows classical players to avoid that buzzing (chasqueo) and pursue a clean, full, bell-like sound.

Flamenco guitar is the more percussive of the two, and it has special techniques not found in classical guitar, such as rajeos, *alzapúa*, and golpe that let flamenco guitarists emphasize the percussive side of the guitar and keep the rhythm fluent and present. In addition, unlike classical *tirando*, where the strings are pulled parallel to the soundboard, in flamenco *apoyando*, strings are struck towards the soundboard in such way that the striking finger is caught and supported by the next finger.

The materials used on a flamenco guitar tend to be thinner. This contributes to a sense of lightness all around, increases volume, and emphasizes the attack. Spruce is the most common used wood in the top of a traditional flamenco guitar (German spruce, most commonly). The spruce has the characteristics of a powerful, brilliant, and direct tone that keeps its clarity when playing strong rajeos and alzapúas.

Thin, lightweight cypress is the most common wood for the back and sides of most traditional flamenco guitars. This type of guitar is called *blanca* ("white"). Cypress creates a brilliant sound and enhances the volume of the guitar, which makes it suitable for accompanying the voice and dance. In addition, it is much cheaper than rosewood (common in classical guitars), which in the early period was not affordable by flamenco musicians.

A classical guitar, contrarily, is built with much heavier and thicker woods. Cedar is the main wood used for the top; it is more rarely found on a flamenco guitar due to its darker, fuller, and less piercing tone.

For the back and the sides, rosewood, maple, and mahogany are the most used woods in a classical guitar. Unlike the brilliantness and lightness of cypress, thicker components made from these denser woods produce a deep, loud, and resonant sound and enhances the sustain of the guitar. Note that there is also a type of flamenco guitar that uses rosewood (*palosanto*) for back and sides. These guitars are called *negras* ("black") and have a more profound and full sound than the blancas (cypress made guitars). Blancas are more suitable for voice and dance accompaniment, and negras are used mainly in a solo concert setting (*guitarra de concierto*).

The most significant physical feature of a flamenco guitar is the tapping plate (*golpeador*), which is almost invariably present in the form of a transparent or white plastic sheet fixed to the soundboard. Tapping plates are made of thin bone or synthetic material to protect the thin surface from the player's fingernails and facilitate the on-soundboard percussion (*golpe*) necessary in flamenco music.

Depending on the instrument, the tapping plate may or may not be visible. In the videos accompanying this book, my guitar is a fine handmade rosewood instrument, with a transparent tapping plate. On higher end instruments like this, the tapping plate is often transparent.

Another interesting feature is the wooden tuning pegs used in vintage flamenco guitars, unlike mechanical tuning pegs used on classical guitars. However, most modern flamenco guitars also have mechanical tuning pegs.

Finally, classical guitar performance is usually based on achieving a clean, deep, nuanced, reverberant, and mellow tone. On the other hand, flamenco guitar performance is characterized by producing a brighter, dryer, punchier, and more percussive sound.

POSTURE AND PERFORMANCE

Early flamenco players held their guitars by placing it on top of their right leg, supporting it with their fretting hand, and with both feet on the ground. This position diminishes the mobility of the fretting hand, which is already busy holding the guitar. However, this was not an issue for traditional flamenco players, because at the time, they only used the "por arriba" (E Phrygian) and "por medio" (A Phrygian) tonalities and played the scales and chords (*posturas*) in the first position of the guitar (first five frets).

Modern flamenco players (beginning with Paco de Lucía) tend to cross their legs and hold the guitar on top of the right leg, in order to gain agility and capability in the fretting hand (as shown in figure I.2). Holding the guitar with the right leg frees the fretting hand to move across the fretboard and reach all positions.

FIG. I.2. Posture (Contemporary)

Your shoulders should be totally relaxed. Your elbow should be placed on the top of the guitar so that your strumming hand can move naturally and freely.

Flamenco guitar is performed by placing the strumming hand between the sound hole and the bridge of the guitar, in order to produce a harsh and rasping sound quality. A clear, round, full sound can also be made in this exact position, but that desired brilliant and percussive flamenco sound is possible here because of the added tension of the strings closer to the bridge.

Place your strumming hand so that the line of your knuckles is nearly parallel to the strings, with your thumb to the left of your fingers. Your hand should be as relaxed as possible. Do not try to force it in any way. Rest your thumb on the sixth string and your fingers perpendicular to the strings. (See figure I.2.)

Keep this fixed (but relaxed) position on your strumming hand. Try to perform every technique by slightly varying this position. It will take some time to master, but in the long term, it will save you a lot of time and effort.

Your fretting hand should also stay relaxed. Keep your fingertips perpendicular to the guitar strings, near the frets. Your thumb and hand stay straight, with a bit of room between your palm and the guitar neck. The thumb of your fretting hand should always be behind the neck. This helps to keep your fretting hand straight.

Again, keep your strumming hand knuckles parallel to the guitar strings, allowing your fingers to come down at an angle to the strings rather than squarely across from them. Your third and fourth fingers will have to travel further to stop the strings. It is crucial to develop the strength, speed, and accuracy to use them effectively in fast picados and ligados (see chapter 2, 8, and 11).

Flamenco guitarists generally use a capo (*cejilla*) in their playing. The capo helps in two main ways. First, it makes the guitar sound sharper and more percussive, because it shortens the effective string lengths, and thus, less of the string is vibrating. The capo applies pressure to the strings, like the first finger in a barre chord. This higher pressure and shorter string length lowers the action and increases the playability of the strings, making the response faster.

The second use for the capo is to allow the guitarist to match a singer's individual vocal range and specific tonality. Rather than transposing a certain flamenco song (*cante*) to the key of the singer (as is common in jazz), flamenco guitarists use the capo as a transposing tool because it lets us retain the sonority of the traditional tonalities (por arriba and por medio) without having to change the traditional chord positions (posturas) and scales.

Before flamenco guitarists started using capos, singers had to adapt their voices to the flamenco guitarists' limited tonalities, rather than guitarists adapting to the singer's wide tonality.

AREAS OF STUDY IN FLAMENCO GUITAR

In order to become a proficient flamenco guitarist (*tocaor*), the aspiring student must master the following three disciplines: solo playing, singing accompaniment, and dance accompaniment.

Solo Playing (*Toque Solista*)

Toque is the term used to refer to the art of flamenco guitar playing. This term is also used for a flamenco palo (form or style) that is performed in a solo guitar setting. The main elements of a toque are the rhythm, harmony, melody, and composition.

Rhythm is the most important element of a toque, and it is grounded on what flamenco musicians call *compás* (which refers to the different rhythmic cycles that are used in flamenco music). Each toque has associated a specific compás/rhythmic cycle, and there is a strong relationship/identification between them (see part I).

The harmony of a toque is developed in a tonal and modal environment, based on the harmonization of the Andalusian cadence (see lesson 3). In addition, the flamenco styles that are grounded in major and minor keys use the perfect and imperfect cadences borrowed from western classical music.

The melodies of the flamenco guitar toques try to emulate the melodies of the voice (*cante*), which have popular origin and have been orally transmitted among artists and the flamenco community. The techniques used by flamenco guitarists to perform melodies are picado (apoyando, for scales); the thumb, thumb/index, or thumb/middle finger; four-note trémolos; and abundant ligados of the fretting hand.

Flamenco guitarists have a unique approach to composition and form. Instead of composing whole tunes, they perform a collection of what is known as "falsetas," which constitute the primary compositional element in flamenco guitar. A falseta is a short variation or micro composition based on a theme that flamenco guitarists originally played between sung verses and dance sections, while the singer breathes or the dancer performs with slow *marcajes* (arm and body movements) or in a percussive way that reinforces your falseta's rhythms, particularly the ending (*cierre* or *remate*). The theme is mainly based on the melody of the cante, and it is generally introduced at the beginning of the falseta (one or two bars long, generally).

After that, guitarists either play a short development or variation of the melody and a powerful ending (*cierre*), similar to how jazz musicians build their solos. The harmony of a falseta is based in the same harmonic principles of the toque discussed above. As in the toques, rhythm (*compás*) is the most important element.

Due to the absence of a clear, written pedagogical tradition in flamenco music, each flamenco guitarist has developed a unique way of composing their own falsetas and toques. The way of learning and teaching them is by direct contact with other guitarists or mentors, and listening to the various recordings available. One listens to the other's falseta, learns it, and potentially makes their own version of it. In order to become a successful soloist, you should have a lot of falsetas on each palo. My advice for the aspiring student is to start by learning the falsetas of the masters mentioned in lesson 4.

As a final comment, before becoming a soloist, it is very important to learn how to accompany songs and dance (*cante* and *baile*). This is crucial and will improve your compás/rhythm and knowledge of the basic structures of flamenco music (as in jazz, you should first learn the standards to learn the language properly).

Chant Accompaniment (*Toque pa Cante*)

Cante directly translates as "song." It is also used among flamenco musicians to refer to palos that are performed with solo voice or guitar and voice. Each *cante* is a broad category that includes lyrics (*letras*) that are generally classified in styles (*estilos*), or subgenres, according to their regional origin (such as *fandangos de Huelva*) or the creator of that particular style (*malagueña de Antonio Chacón*).

The letras are sung lyric lines (*tercios*) that have popular origin and constitute the literary and poetic part of flamenco music. Like falsetas, the letras have been orally transmitted through the direct contact between artists and among the flamenco community. Letras normally conform to strophe/stanza types (*estrofas*), which have been part of Spanish (and general European) literature and folk music for centuries before flamenco appeared. Figure I.3 describes three of the most common estrofas found in flamenco literature.

Types of Estrofas	Description
Tercerilla	Three lines with eight syllables per line.
Copla	Four lines (*cuarteta*) with eight syllables per line.
Quintilla	Five lines with eight syllables per line. This is the estrofa of all fandangos.

FIG. I.3. Types of Estrofas

Typically, within a cante, flamenco singers mix and match letras of their choosing (with different themes), in whatever order they want, as opposed to singing a complete song where the verses follow a particular order and theme. In addition, the flamenco lyrics are not usually sung as they are conceived. Singers frequently repeat verses, connect the end of a verse with the following one, or repeat words of a verse in order to adapt it to the music and inspiration of the moment.

The role of the accompanying guitarist is to maintain the compás (rhythmic cycle), harmonize the vocal melody, and give answers (call-response phrases) to the voice, rather than showing off the guitarist's playing and technical abilities. Occasionally, between letras, the guitarist might also play a falseta or *detalle* (like a fill), to inspire the singer or to allow them to breathe.

Often, there is no prior rehearsal with the singer, so you should already have a collection of falsetas and response phrases, and know the underlying harmony associated with the different styles of letras, in order to accompany singers in real time. The singer will just tell you the palo they will sing, where to put your capo, and whether it will be played "por medio" or "por arriba," (with expressions such as "*al cinco por arriba*," to mean that the capo is on the fifth fret and it is in E Phrygian, or *"al cuatro por medio,"* with the capo on the fourth fret, in A Phrygian). Then, after your introduction, the singer will start singing a collection of letras in different styles (*estilos*), occasionally indicating (with a gesture) when it is time for a falseta.

The singer will often vary the melody and rhythmic accentuation of a letra according to their personality and inspiration of the moment, so we guitarists must adapt our playing (dynamics, texture, strength…) to the personality and character of each singer in real time. This means that you have to observe the singer and support them during the whole cante, rather than playing long falsetas or trying to show your technical abilities. (The solo playing discipline of flamenco is a more suitable context for that.)

To become a great cante accompanist, you must become familiar with the cantes, letras, and styles that represent the main aspects of flamenco music (see chapter 4). I also recommend that you sing them while accompanying yourself, even if you are not an experienced singer. This will help you get in the mindset of the singer/cantaor.

Dance Accompaniment (*Toque pa Baile*)

Baile means "dance." This term is also used to refer to a *palo* that is performed with guitar, voice, and dance. When accompanying a dancer (*bailaor*/*bailaora*), the flamenco guitarist must be familiar with the letras and styles (the singer will sing during the baile), and with all the inner formal parts of the different *bailes* (danceable flamenco forms).

Flamenco dancers have developed a unique terminology for these parts, as well as a unique way of communicating them to the singer (cantaor) and the guitarist (tocaor). See lesson 4 for more information about baile form.

There are two main performance situations that the flamenco guitarist will face when working with a dancer. If we are performing with a big dancing company, such as Sara Baras or Joaquín Cortés, then all the parts of the baile will be carefully composed, rehearsed, and structured before the show. The guitar player composes specific music for the baile created by the dancer, where in addition to the specific cuts (*cortes*) and endings (*remate*) of each part of the baile, lighting or scenography of the live show are also taken into account.

Alternatively, when you perform in a *tablao* or a *peña* (traditional bars that feature flamenco performances), there are no rehearsals when playing with a dancer, so you must be prepared to react and improvise with them. This requires that you already know a collection of falsetas (short guitar phrases and variations) suitable for dance in each flamenco musical form. In addition, you must have an extensive knowledge of all the styles of song (cante/letras) and dance parts (baile), almost to the extent of being able to sing them. Then you will be ready to accompany and improvise.

Improvisation in flamenco music is basically based on form—not form as in jazz, where we play (for example) a 32-bar form AABA and improvise over a chord progression. Form in flamenco refers to the order in which the elements of the baile appear throughout the performance. The singer might sing a letra, the dancer might perform a llamada or escobilla, and the guitarist might play a falseta. The others must pay attention and react in the moment. For this formula to succeed, each of the three elements—song/dance/guitar solo—must be put forth as a unique stand-alone performance, in order to produce a symbiosis that optimizes the final result.

Accompanying a dancer is considered the first step in the career of a flamenco guitarist (playing in a tablao). The way of learning this discipline is to play with dancers. You must have a strong compás/rhythm, a well-developed rajeo (main technique used to accompany the dancer´s footwork), intuition, and deep knowledge of singing styles and bailes structures (see lesson 4).

Flamenco guitarists generally specialize in one of these three disciplines. However, every flamenco guitarist should have fluency in all three of them.

"Muy Especial" by La Moneta, 2017. Guitar: Luís Mariano; Singer: Juan Ángel Tirado; Dancer: La Moneta. Photo by Beatrix Mexi Molnar.

PART I

Theory and Concepts

On the way to becoming flamenco guitarists, there are certain aspects that we must practice. Guitarists who are new to the genre often focus all their efforts and time in technical study, trying to gain speed and strength in their playing. Of course, the technical aspect of the guitar is very important, and in the later sections of this book, you will learn flamenco guitar techniques and then apply them to practical etudes and exercises, in order to develop your abilities.

As important as technique is, it is the rhythms (compás), harmonies, and forms of the different flamenco styles or palos that distinguish the genre. Rhythm is the main element of both flamenco and Spanish music generally, and without compás (rhythmic feel), everything we do on the guitar will be of little value.

It is often said that flamenco is an improvised music. However, it has a strong structure, which dancers (bailaora/or), guitarists (tocaora/or), and singers (cantaora/or) all respect and follow throughout the performance. Likewise, flamenco has characteristic cadences, chords, and scales that make the music recognizable as flamenco anywhere in the world.

In this section, we will look closely at the conceptual and theoretical characteristics that make flamenco unique.

CHAPTER 1

Rhythmic Cycles in Flamenco Music

Compás is the Spanish word for meter or time signature. In flamenco, besides having these meanings, it also refers to the rhythmic cycle, or layout of a palo (flamenco form). It also commonly means just "rhythm," in expressions such as "*tener compás*" (to have rhythm) or "*tocar a compás*" (to play in rhythm). *Soniquete* refers to the mastery of rhythm/compás.

In order to improve the compás and soniquete in our playing, practice the most common clapping (*palmas*) and foot (*pie*) patterns of each palo before playing the guitar part (shown below). This is a common practice that singers, dancers, and guitarists do as a preliminary rhythm study, in order to internalize the compás/rhythmic cycle types as well as the variety of accents contained in them.

Flamenco palos may be in ternary or binary meter, sometimes with hemiola structures.

TERNARY STYLES

Spanish (mainly Andalusian) popular music is usually in ternary meter (sets of three beats), such as the classic 3/4. The main palos that are derived from this category are fandangos de huelva, fandangos abandolaos, and sevillanas.

Classic Ternary-Style Flamenco Recordings		
Song	**Palo**	**Artist**
"Al Niño Miguel"	Fandangos de Huelva	Rafael Riqueni
"Vengo de los Montes"	Fandango Abandolao	Fosforito
"Sevilla"	Sevillanas	Gerardo Núñez

Let's practice the main clapping and foot pattern on a fandangos de huelva. Note that there are two types of flamenco claps:

1. ***Palmas sordas***, a muffled clap made with cupped hands.
2. ***Palmas abiertas***, a dry clap made with the palms of open hands.

In addition to the claps, the patterns are also punctuated by the *pie*, a tap made with the foot.

Track 1 is made with palmas abiertas and track 2 with palmas sordas, so that you can hear the difference in sound.

1, 2

Fandangos de Huelva

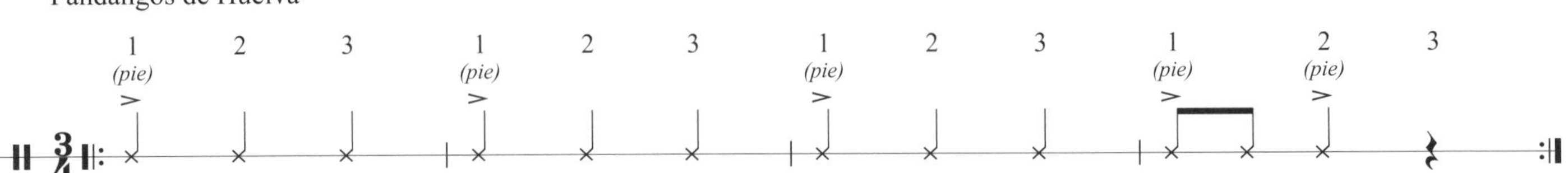

FIG. 1.1. Ternary Rhythmic Pattern: Fandangos de Huelva

BINARY STYLES

There are many palos that are in a binary meter, performed in 2/4 or 4/4. In flamenco, the binary meter comes from the habanera pattern. It is typical in tangos and many tango variations, such as tientos, rumba, farruca, garrotín, mariana, zambra, and taranto.

Classic Binary-Style Flamenco Recordings		
Song	**Palo**	**Artist**
"Rosa María"	Tangos	Camarón de la Isla
"De la Vera"	Garrotín	Rafael Riqueni
"Entre dos Aguas"	Rumba	Paco de Lucía

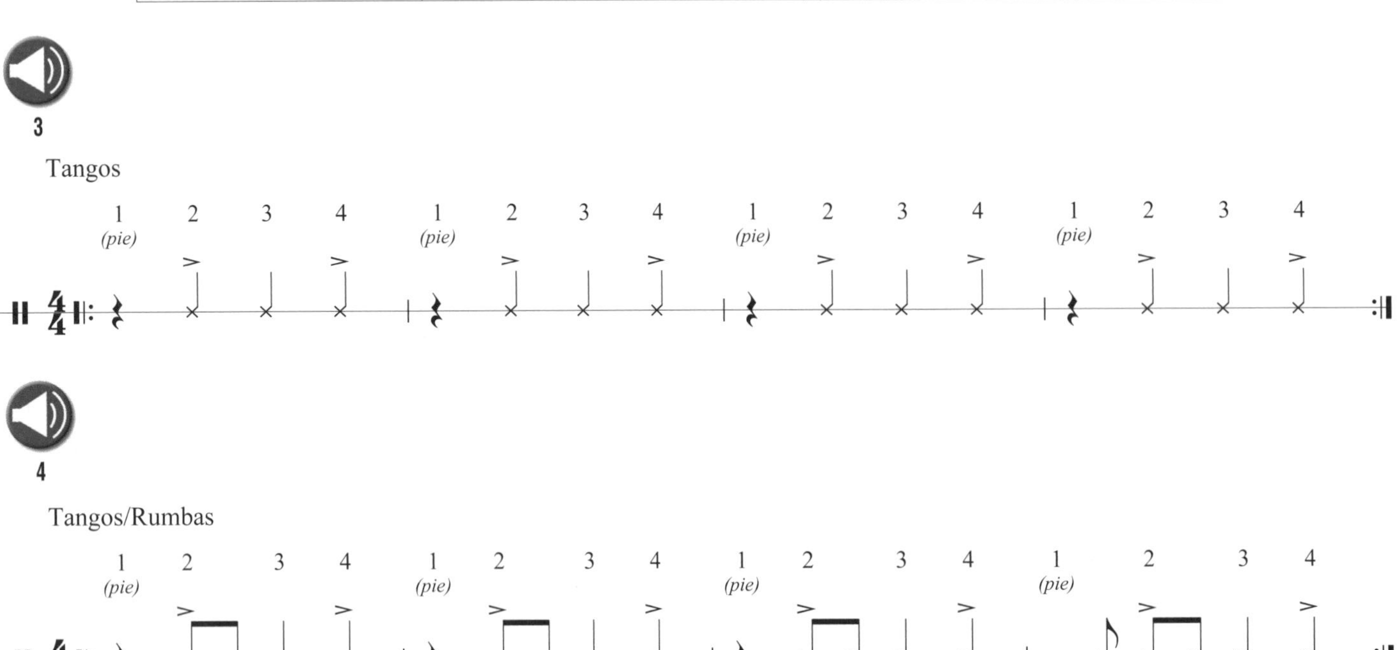

FIG. 1.2. Binary Patterns: (a) Tangos (b) Rumbas

HEMIOLA

Hemiola is the most genuine, most characteristic pattern employed in flamenco music, and each palo has a characteristic hemiola pattern. A hemiola is based on the alternation of a binary measure notated in 6/8 with a ternary measure in 3/4. Combined, these two measures include twelve eighth-note subdivisions.

Flamenco dancers developed a unique way of counting the twelve-part hemiola, renaming notes 1 and 2 as 2 and 1, and renaming the ending notes 11 and 12 as 10 and 1.

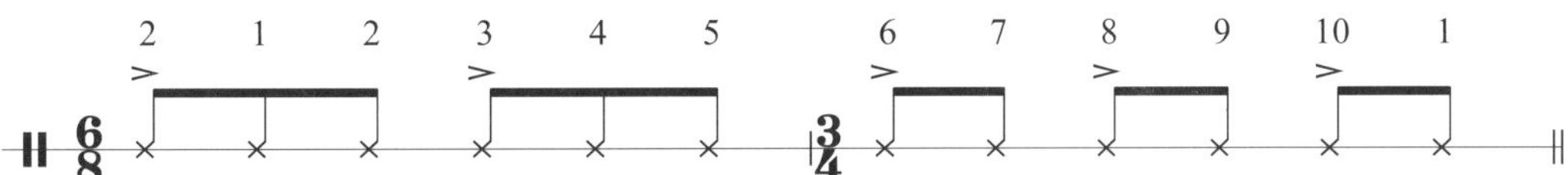

FIG. 1.3. Counting a Hemiola Pattern

Classic Flamenco Recordings Featuring Hemiola		
Song	**Palo**	**Artist**
"La Puerta del Príncipe"	Alegrías	Manolo Sanlúcar
"Antonia"	Soleá por Bulerías	Paco de Lucía
"Bulerías de Jeréz"	Bulerías	Terremoto de Jerez
"El Mundo es un Desengaño"	Soleá	Chocolate

Here are the hemiola patterns used in several different palos. The pattern in figure 1.4 is used in the alegrías and soleá por bulerías. This same pattern is also used in soleá (track 6), but slower.

5, 6

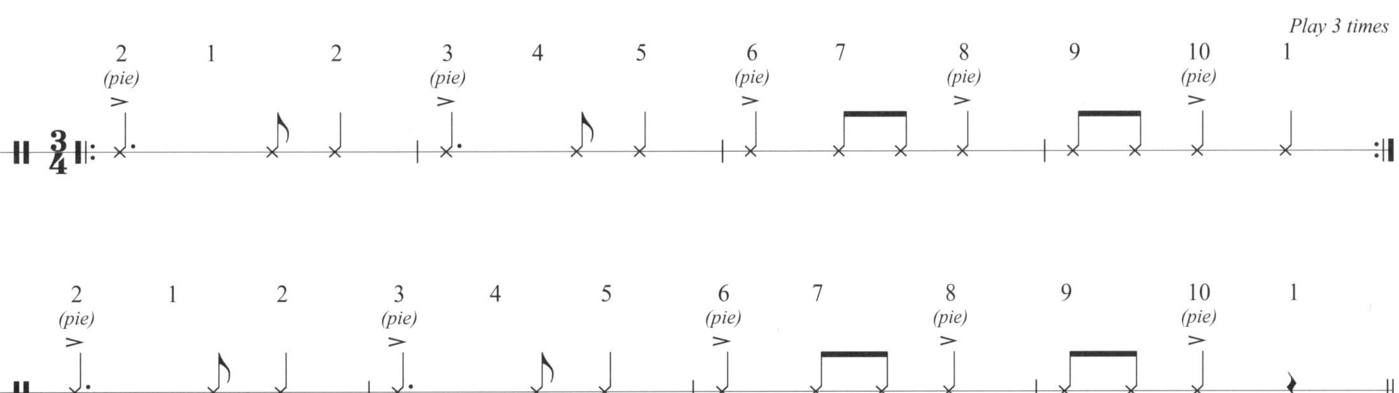

FIG. 1.4. Hemiola Pattern for Alegrías, Soleá por Bulerías, and Soleá

For the bulerías pattern, first practice the three examples in tracks 7, 8, and 9 separately. They are performed simultaneously, as in track 10.

7

Bulerías I

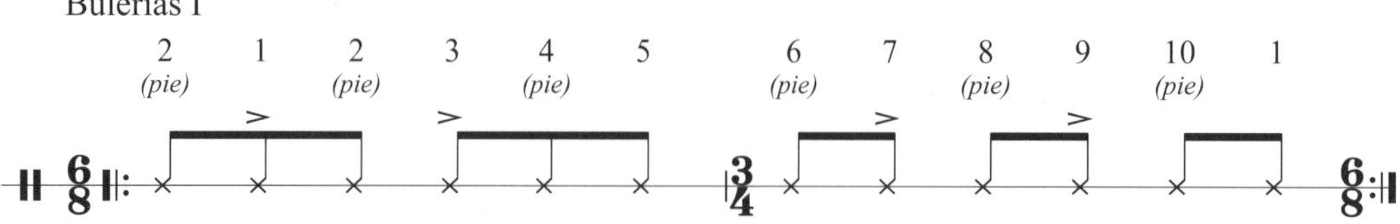

8

Bulerías II

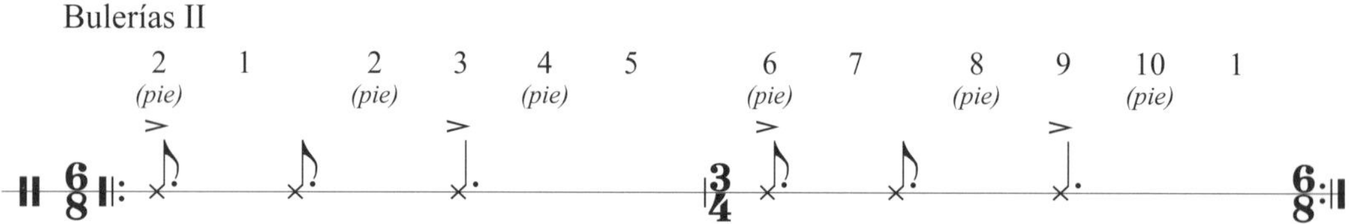

9

Bulerías III

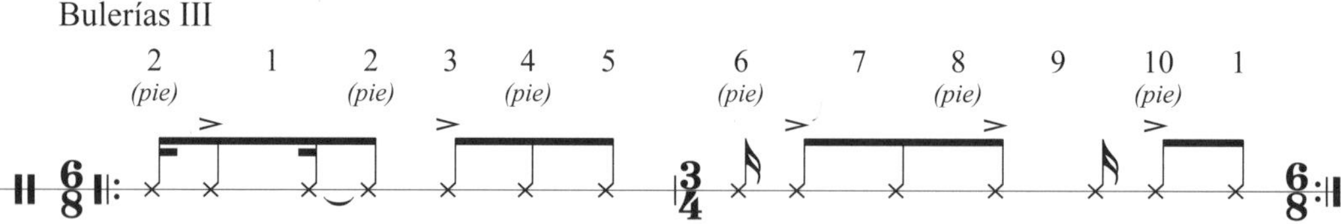

FIG. 1.5. Hemiola Patterns for Bulerías

Try recording the three bulerías patterns of figure 1.5 together, and listen to how it sounds.

10

In the seguiriyas palo, flamenco musicians count the five main accents, as shown in figure 1.6. This twelve-beat structure is the same as the pattern used in soleá or bulerías (figure 1.5) but starting on beat 8 and accenting beats **8** 9 **10** 11 **12** 1 2 **3** 4 5 **6** 7.

11

Seguiriya

Play 3 times

1 / 2 / 3 / / 4 / / 5 /
(pie) (pie) (pie) (pie) (pie)

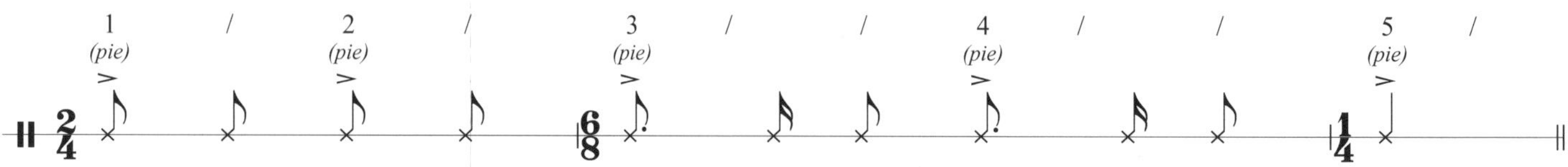

FIG. 1.6. Hemiola Pattern in Seguiriya

ESTILOS LIBRES

Estilos libres ("free styles") refers to the flamenco musical forms in which there is not a recognizable meter. However, most of the free styles belong to the family of fandangos, so they have an inner ternary feel. When playing a solo guitar piece in estilos libres, it is called a "toque libre."

Classic Toques Libres Flamenco Recordings		
Song	**Palo**	**Artist**
"La Cartuja"	Granaína	Gerardo Núñez
"Fuente y Caudal"	Taranta	Paco de Lucía
"Villarosa"	Minera	Rafael Riqueni

In the category of cantes that are in estilos libres, we also find several singing styles that are interpreted without guitar accompaniment, known as *a palo seco* styles, where the voice is the only instrument.

Classic a Palo Seco Flamenco Recordings		
Song	**Palo**	**Artist**
"Ay nadie diga que"	Martinete	Manuel Agujetas
"Yo no te obligo gitana de que"	Toná	Antonio Mairena

"Café Cantante" (Café de el Burrero), Seville (Spain), 1888. Photo by Emilio Beauchy Cano. In this photo are la Rubia de Málaga, Juanaca de Málaga, José León "La Escribana," Concha "La Carbonera," Silverio Franconetti, Pepa de Oro, La Serrana, La Sordita y Fernanda Antúnez, La Melliza, Dolores Pérez, and Gabriela Ortega; the rest are unknown.

CHAPTER 2

Flamenco Chords and Scales

Genuine flamenco sonority is generated by the family of chords that contain the ♭9. Among them, the most used chords are the following, both "por arriba" (in E Phrygian) and "por medio" (in A Phrygian). It is also common to find the 7 of the A7(♭9) chord (G) placed in the root (sixth string), as in bar 4.

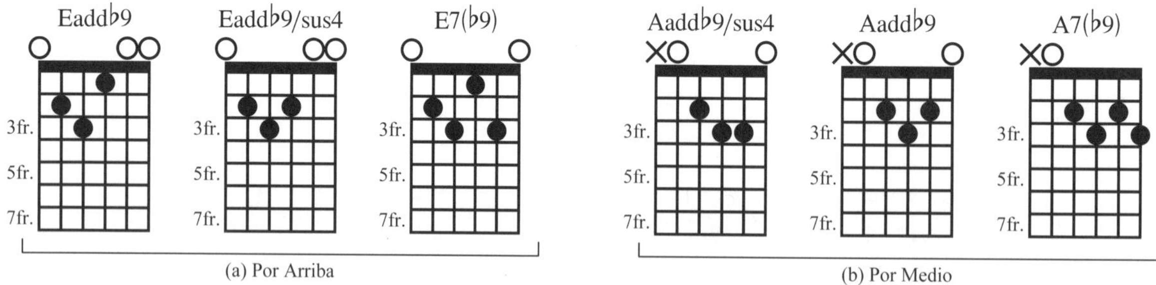

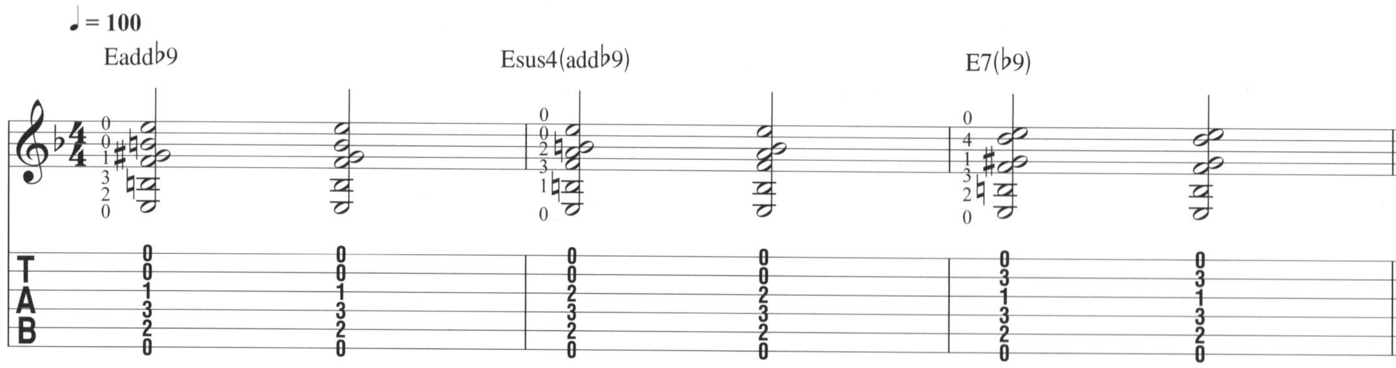

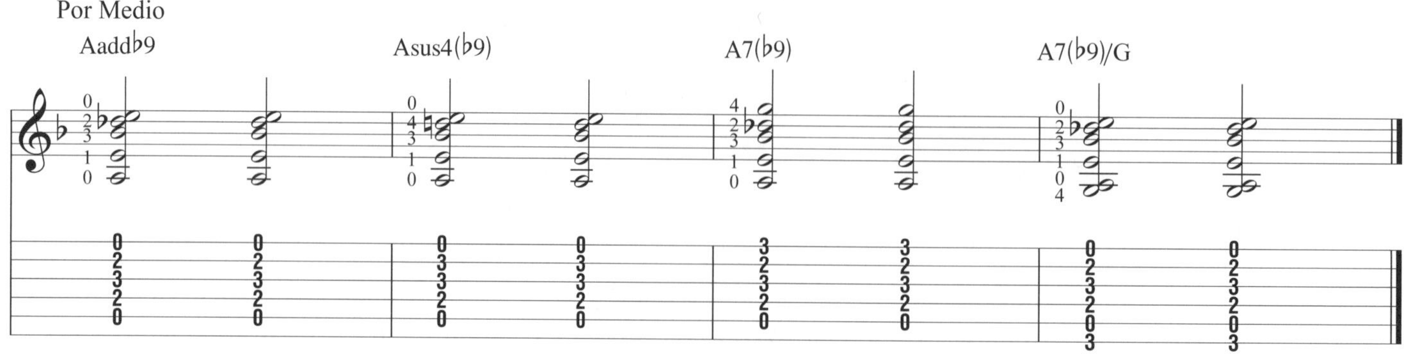

FIG. 2.1. Flamenco Chords with ♭9: (a) por arriba [in E Phrygian] (b) por medio [in A Phrygian]

The most common scales that flamenco musicians use for these chords are the Phrygian and Phrygian dominant scales.

13 2

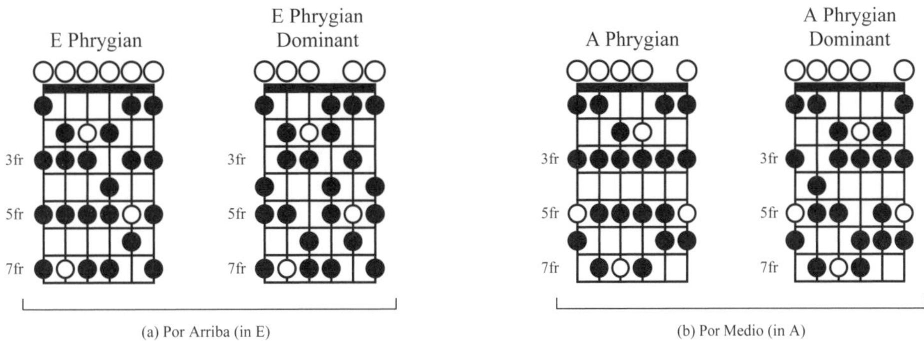

FIG. 2.2. Common Scale Fingerings: Phrygian and Phrygian Dominant in E and A

SCALE EXERCISES

(a) Por Arriba

♩ = 100 bpm

i m i m

6

i m i m

10

i m i m

15

i m i m

(b) Por Medio

FIG. 2.3. Scale Fingering Exercise

CHAPTER 3

Andalusian Cadence

The Andalusian cadence is a sequence of four chords that are characteristic of Spanish and flamenco music.

Let's play the Andalusian cadence in the two traditional flamenco tonalities: por arriba and por medio. For the last chord, flamenco guitarists mainly use either major, dominant 7, add♭9, add♭9(sus4), or 7(♭9) voicings.

14, 15

3, 4

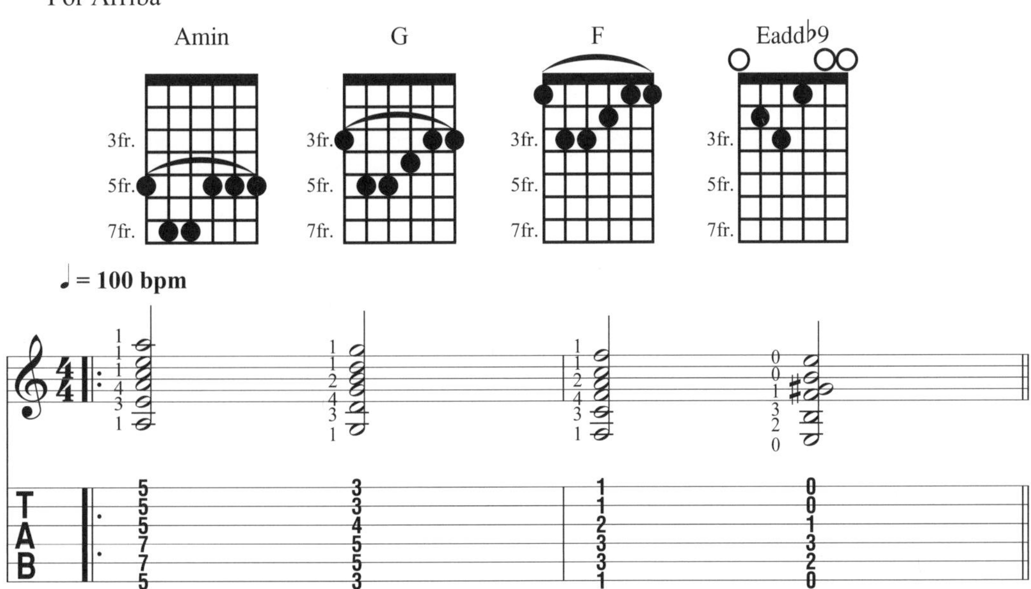

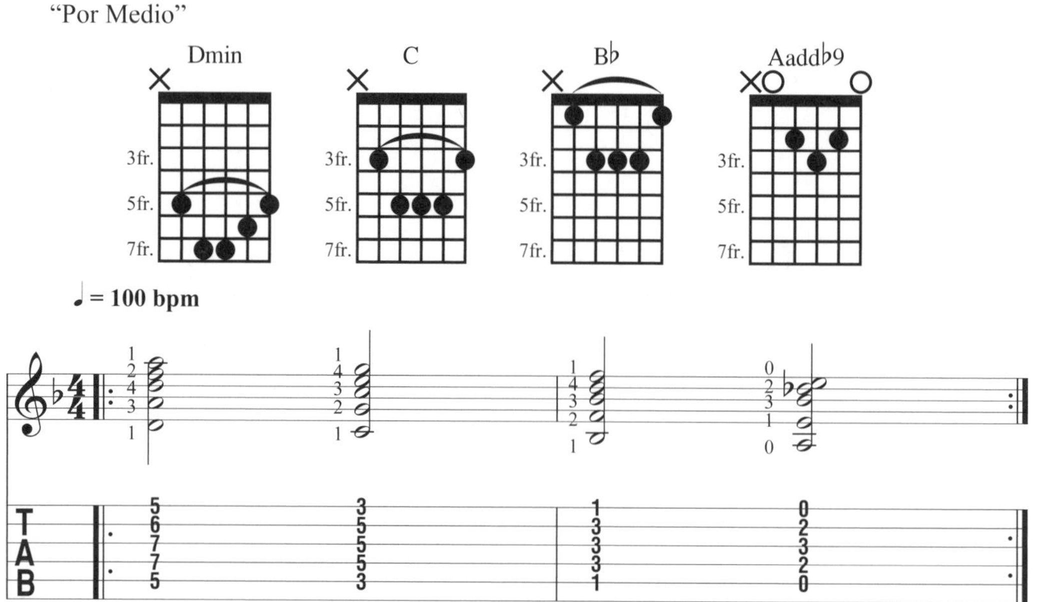

FIG. 3.1. Andalusian Cadences: Por Arriba and Por Medio

During the first half of the 20th century, the master Ramón Montoya introduced the Andalusian cadence in B (*granaína*), F♯ (*taranta*), and G♯ (*minera*) Phrygian. Continuing this path, the generation led by Paco de Lucía, Manolo Sanlúcar, and Serranito introduced the C♯, D, and D♯ Phrygian tonalities.

CHAPTER 4

Forms and Palos

The palos are the different forms/styles of flamenco music. Each palo has characteristic tonalities, rhythmic patterns, melodies, lyrics (letras or cantes), and harmonic sequences. Part III of this book includes etudes of falsetas based on seven common palos.

Figure 4.1 shows a simplified way of identifying the main palos according to these parameters.

Palo	Tonality	Rhythmic Cycle	Characteristic Chord Progressions	BPM
Soleá	E Phrygian	12-Beat Pattern	E7alt F E7alt	90
Fandangos de Huelva	E Phrygian	3/4 Pattern	E7alt Ami G7 F E7alt	140
Guajira	A Ionian	12-Beat Pattern	E7 A	175
Bulerías	A Phrygian	12-Beat Pattern	A7alt B♭ A7alt	120
Alegrías	C, A, or E Ionian	12-Beat Pattern	G7 C B7 E E7 A	150
Tangos	A Phrygian	4/4 Pattern	B♭ A7alt	145
Rumbas	A Aeolian	4/4 Pattern	Ami G7 F E7alt	190
Soleá por Bulerías	A Phrygian	12-Beat Pattern	A7alt B♭ A7alt	140
Granaína	B Phrygian	n/a	Emi7 D7 C7 B7alt	n/a
Minera	G♯ Phrygian	n/a	G♯7alt A7♭5 G♯7alt	n/a
Taranta	F♯ Phrygian	n/a	F♯7alt G7 F♯7alt	n/a
Seguiriya	A Phrygian	12-Beat Pattern	Dmi C7 B♭ A7alt	125

FIG. 4.1. Characteristics of Common Palos. Examples of the first seven palo types are found in part III.

SOLO GUITAR (TOQUE SOLISTA)

A *toque solista*, or solo guitar piece, can last for about five to seven minutes. The format is a collection of falsetas performed one after the other that together give a sense of unity throughout the piece.

A falseta is a variation based on a cante's melody—a micro composition about 30 to 60 seconds long, with a recognizable melody (based on the cante), a short development, and a powerful rhythmic ending (cierre). Falsetas are the melodic aspect of flamenco guitar that is different from playing raw rhythm/compás. The different falsetas included in a toque are not necessarily connected melodically, but they all must share the same character of the palo/toque.

Here are some examples of some of my own falsetas, introduced by the palos for which they were written. We explore them in more depth in part III.

Toques Solistas by Yago Santos		
Song	**Palo**	**Video Track**
"Falseta I"	Soleá Por Bulerías	89
"Falseta II"	Bulerías	82
"Falseta III"	Soleá	71
"A Fali"	Soleá Por Bulerías	95

Here is the form I used for "A Fali," a soleá por bulerías (track 5).

5

Introduction	Falseta 1	Falseta 2	Falseta 3	Falseta 4	Falseta 5	Cierre

FIG. 4.2. Form for "A Fali" Toque Solista

- This introduction is free—ad libitum, not attached to the compás.
- Between the introduction and the first falseta, I play a couple bars of raw compás.
- This toque includes five falsetas. Falseta 5 increases the tempo, leading us to the cierre.
- Cierre is the ending. They generally have a strong rhythmic feel.

An example of a free toque is "Calle de la Memoria," a taranta (track 6).

6

Before composing your own falsetas and toques, learn the falsetas of the four primary masters of flamenco guitar: Ramón Montoya, Niño Ricardo, Sabicas, and Paco de Lucía. Once you know some of them, start by varying those falsetas, as the next step towards creating your own.

SONG (CANTE)

When accompanying a singer (cantaor/cantaora), the structure of a palo combines the lyrics (letras) sung by the singer with call-and-response phrases (*respuestas al cante*) and falsetas played by the guitarist (tocaor).

Here is one possible overall structure of a complete cante.

Guitar Introduction	Salida del Cante	Detalle	Letra 1	Letra 2	Falseta	Letra 3	Macho	Remate / Cierre

FIG. 4.3. Example Structure of a Cante

The guitar introduction sets the tone and mood of the palo. *Salida del cante* is where the singer tunes their voice (*temple*), generally with an "Ay," "Lere," or "Tiritítran." The singer uses this section to warm up and get the feel of the framework of the tonality and scale of the cante.

Detalles are guitar-focused interludes, generally one or one-half measures long, to give space for the cantaor to breathe, after the temple or between letras.

For a falseta to be suitable for a cante, it should not be too long and never overshadow or intrude upon the singer. Remember that the guitar is just accompanying the voice or serving as an answer to the vocal part. Listen to the falsetas *pa cante* created by Niño Ricardo, Melchor de Marchena, Diego del Gastor, and Juan Habichuela in order to familiarize yourself with the essence of toque pa cante.

Macho refers to the last letra of the cante before the ending (remate/cierre), and it is normally the bravest one.

Remate is an ending or tag in some styles. In cantes, these may include a "coletilla," "coro," or "juguetillo." It is performed at a faster tempo and in the parallel major tonality (such as from A Phrygian to A Ionian).

Be aware that the structure in figure 4.3 is not the only possible form for a cante. There are multiple variations, but this is as a starting point.

Here is an example of an actual letra/lyric and a macho sung in soleá form (twelve-beat pattern). This type of letra is a *copla*—a four-line strophe (four *tercios*), with each line including eight syllables.

Note that in lines 1 and 3, the chord changes happen in beat 3 and 10 of the compás. In lines 2 and 4, the Andalusian cadence chords Amin G F are played on beats 1, 2, and 3, and E7alt closes on beat 10.

Spanish	English
E7alt Amin *No sé porqué te resistes*	**E7alt Amin** *I don't know why you resist*
Amin G F E7alt *Si sabes que yo te quiero*	**Amin G F E7alt** *If you know that I love you*
G7 C *Yo sé que no es imposible*	**G7 C** *I know it's not impossible*
Amin G F E7alt *Hacer de la nieve fuego*	**Amin G F E7alt** *Making snow fire*

FIG. 4.4. Letra in Soleá Form

This macho uses a *tercerilla*—a strophe of three lines (tercios), each with eight syllables.

E7alt Amin *Que no te deseo ná,* **G7 C** *Tan solo que tú te mueras* **Amin G F E7alt** *Y yo te vea pasar*	**E7alt Amin** *I don't wish you anything* **G7 C** *Only that you die* **Amin G F E7alt** *And I see you go by*

FIG. 4.5. Macho in Soleá Form

Classic Cantes Recordings		
Song	**Palo**	**Artist**
"Tengo el Gusto Tan Colmado"	Soleá	Tomás Pavón
"Siempre por los Rincones"	Seguiriyas	Manuel Torre
"Matilde la Chula"	Bulerías	La Niña de los Peines

Other great flamenco singers you should listen to are Antonio Chacón and Antonio Mairena (traditional), and Enrique Morente and Camarón de la Isla (contemporary).

DANCE (BAILE)

When playing with a dancer, the structure of the palos is quite different. Each palo is now choreographed (*montaje*), made up of several inner formal elements or passages that give a structural coherence to the palo/baile.

Figure 4.6 describes the most common parts of a baile.

Parts of a Baile	Explanation
Salida (Exit)	The moment where the dancer begins.
Llamada (Call)	Part of the dance that signals the cantaor to start the cante. Also used to signal other changes in the dance.
Marcaje (Marking)	A dancer's way to accompany the singer and the guitarist, accentuating the most important parts of the cante or the falseta.
Zapateado (Tap Dance)	Dance steps (with the feet only).
Escobilla (Broom)	Specific set of dance steps and guitar melody used in the bailes.
Subida (Rise)	Part of the dance that progressively increases in volume and speed.
Cierre (Closing)	Conclusion of a part of the dance.
Desplante (Affront)	Attitude or character that is given to the final pose of a passage.
Remate (Ending)	The ending of a particular letra, falseta, or dance step.
Coletilla (Tag Line)	Lyric/letra that accompanies the end of a dance. It is normally four measures long.

FIG. 4.6. Parts of a Baile

Some of these parts can be found in all the bailes, such as the salida, letras, falsetas, escobilla, and macho.

Some bailes have some unique features, such as the *silencio*—a beautiful guitar interlude played in the parallel minor key—which is used in the alegrías, but rarely found in any other palo/bailes.

A baile generally starts slow and goes faster and faster, but it can also start fast, depending on the dancer. Normally, the escobilla reaches a climactic point, where they either change into a *subida* (speed up faster), or signal the ending with a *llamada* and finish with a remate or cierre.

Here is a typical form of a whole baile (palo to be performed with a dancer), in alegrías form.

Guitar Introduction	Salida del Cante	Salida del Baile	Llamada y Cierre	Letra 1 y Coletilla	Llamada y Cierre	Falseta 1
Letra 2	Llamada/ Cierre	Silencio	Escobilla	Subida/ Llamada	Cierre (optional)	Bulerías de Cádiz

FIG. 4.7. Example Form for a Baile

The guitar introduction is where the guitarist sets the tone of the baile, playing rajeos or an introductory falseta. *Salida del baile* is when the dancer starts to dance. Note that the dancer can also start the baile during the introductory falseta, doing some slow *marcajes*, *braceos*, or *paseos*.

A *llamada* is a specific set of footwork that lets the dancer communicate to the guitar player and singer that a part of the choreography is about to change or end. In the moment that a dancer performs a llamada, the guitar player should accompany the dancer´s footwork with strumming chords and following the dancer's cierre or remate.

The remate represents the end of a particular part of a dance, whether it is a falseta, a letra, or an improvised dance. During the letras, the guitar player should keep the compás, and accompany and harmonize the melodies of the singer, as well as the footwork and accents of the dancer. For the remate of a letra, the guitarist and dancer follow the singer's accentuation. The letras can also be sung one after the other with no remate in between them.

The *escobilla* is a specific dance step and guitar tune that occurs in most bailes. (For examples of escobilla por Alegrías, see part II's "Arpegio Palo Etude: Alegrías" and "Alegrias Falseta II.") It is an important part of the choreography. The ending of the baile alegrías is generally performed in bulerias de cádiz. This is the remate of the baile. It increases in tempo, and while the singer sings, the dancer leaves the stage.

Some great dancers you should check out are Antonio Gades, Mario Maya, Carmen Amaya, and El Farruco.

PART II

Flamenco Guitar Techniques

Before practicing repertoire, I recommend that you warm up for 15 to 30 minutes focusing on technique, in order to gain agility and accuracy in your playing. The functional exercises in this section will help you to improve your left-hand/right-hand coordination.

Start by practicing these exercises slowly, and speed up gradually.

Your goal should be to produce the characteristic sound of each technique, rather than to play quickly. Slow practice is the key to fast playing—and more importantly, to achieving a great sound.

FLAMENCO GUITAR NOTATION SYMBOLS

Normally, when notating flamenco guitar, we use the following symbols. The techniques referenced are discussed in part II.

① ② ③ ④ ⑤ ⑥	Circled numerals indicate strings, with 1 being the highest string (high E in common tuning) and 6 being the lowest string (low E in common tuning).
1 2 3 4	Numerals indicate left-hand (fretboard hand) fingers: 1 index, 2 middle, 3 ring, 4 pinky.
p i m a (e)	Letters indicate right-hand (strumming/plucking hand) fingerings: *p* thumb (*pulgar*), *i* index, *m* middle, *a* ring (*anular*), and more rarely, *e* pinky (*meñique*).
Capo al X	Capo fret location, where X (a Roman numeral) represents the fret number.
C	Barre: Flattening of the fretboard-hand index finger to barre multiple strings.
Ç	Partial barre. On small bar chords, we sometimes find numbers beside the Ç indicating how many strings are to be barred, such as Ç234 for strings ② ③ ④ or Ç 1–5 for strings ① ② ③ ④ ⑤. For example, on the A major chord, you might see Ç34 indicating that you should barre strings ③ ④ with the index finger (1) and place the middle finger (2) on string ②.
□	(*Golpe*). Tap on the guitar top below the first string with middle and ring fingers.
↑	Rajeos (strum) upward, bass to treble, from string ⑥ to string ①.
↓	Rajeos (strum) downward, treble to bass, from string ① to string ⑥.
	Arpeggiated chord.
p	Arpegios: Arpeggiated chord with thumb.
>	Accents: Play the indicated note relatively loudly.
	Stem only (no notehead): Indicates a repeated chord in the rhythm shown.

CHAPTER 5

Golpe

Golpe means a strike or a hit. When we perform this technique, we hit the guitar on the tapping plate (*golpeador*) with our ring and/or middle fingers to create an accent or a percussion effect.

Start by performing the golpe by itself with your ring or middle finger. Make sure that your thumb finger is apoyando (resting) on the sixth string.

Pivot your hand from your thumb, and strike your middle or index finger on the tapping plate (practice both). Keep all your fingers relaxed and curved.

FIG. 5.1. Golpe Practice Strokes

Once you become familiar with this basic motion, you can perform the following exercises, in which you will combine the golpe technique with the index finger and thumb.

GOLPE WARMUP EXERCISES

Golpe Warmup I

16 7

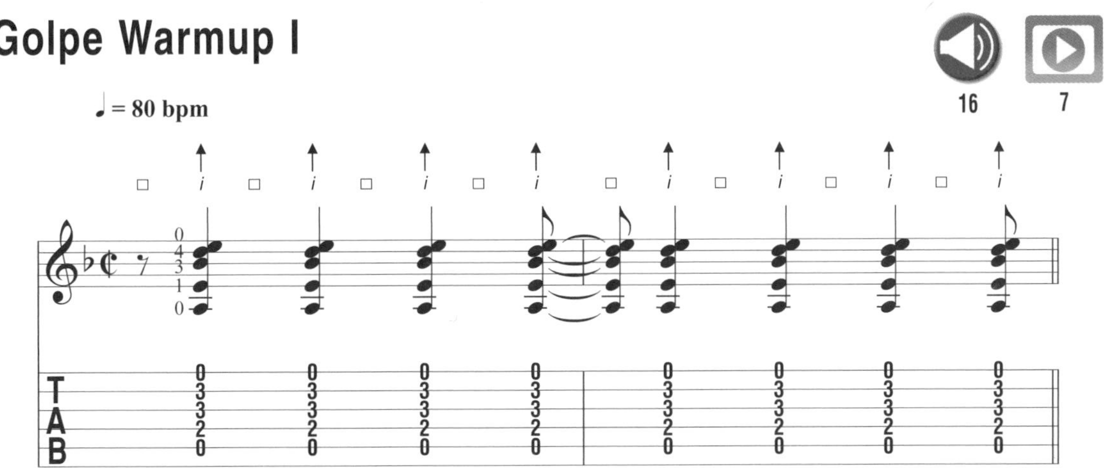

Golpe Warmup II

17 8

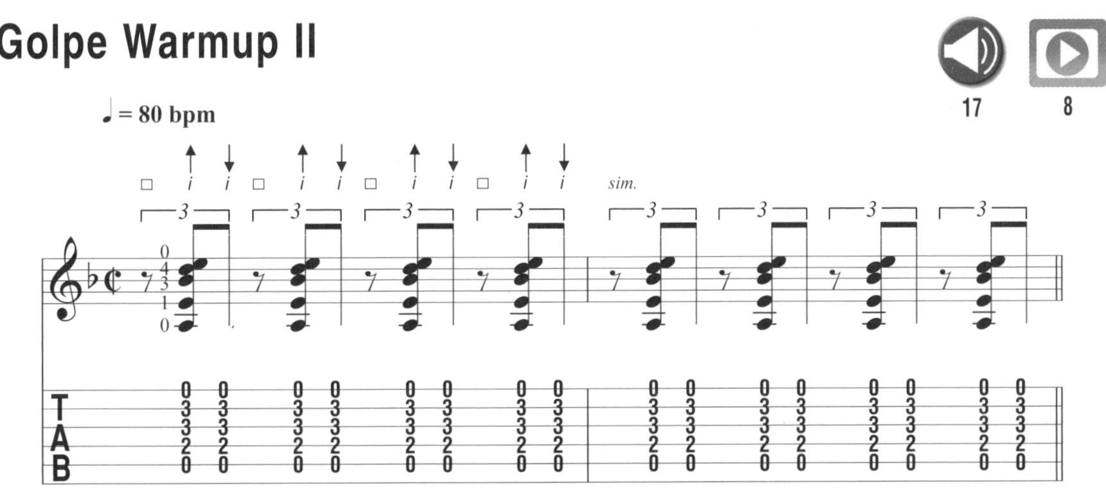

Golpe Warmup III

18 9

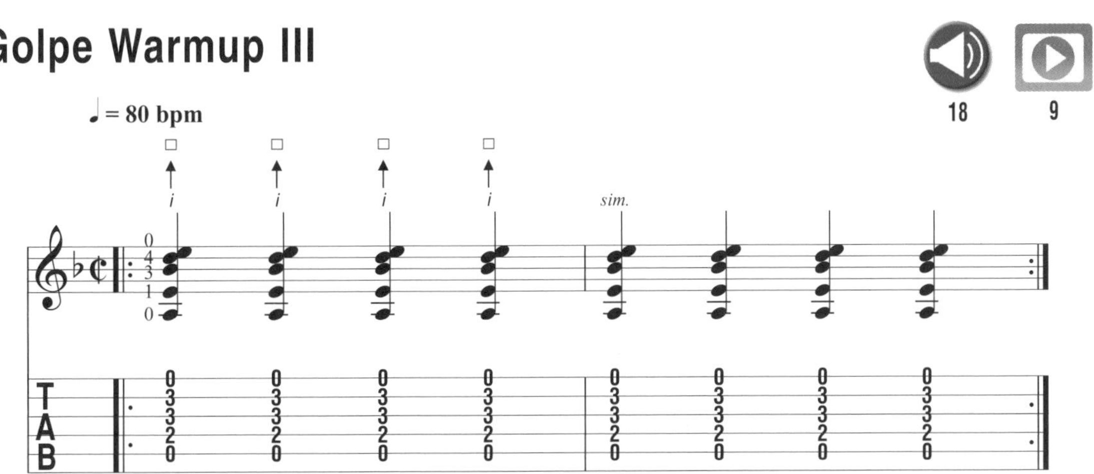

Golpe Warmup IV

19 10

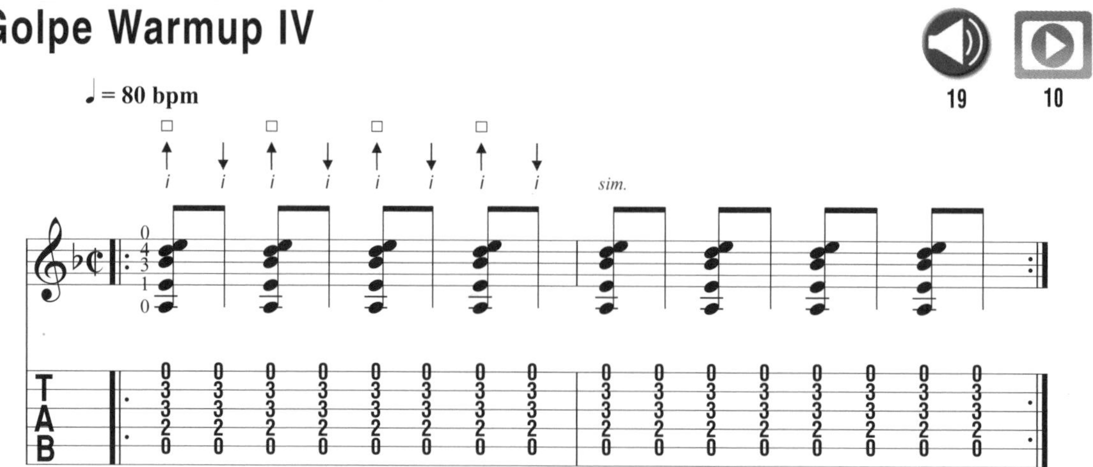

Golpe Warmup V

20 11

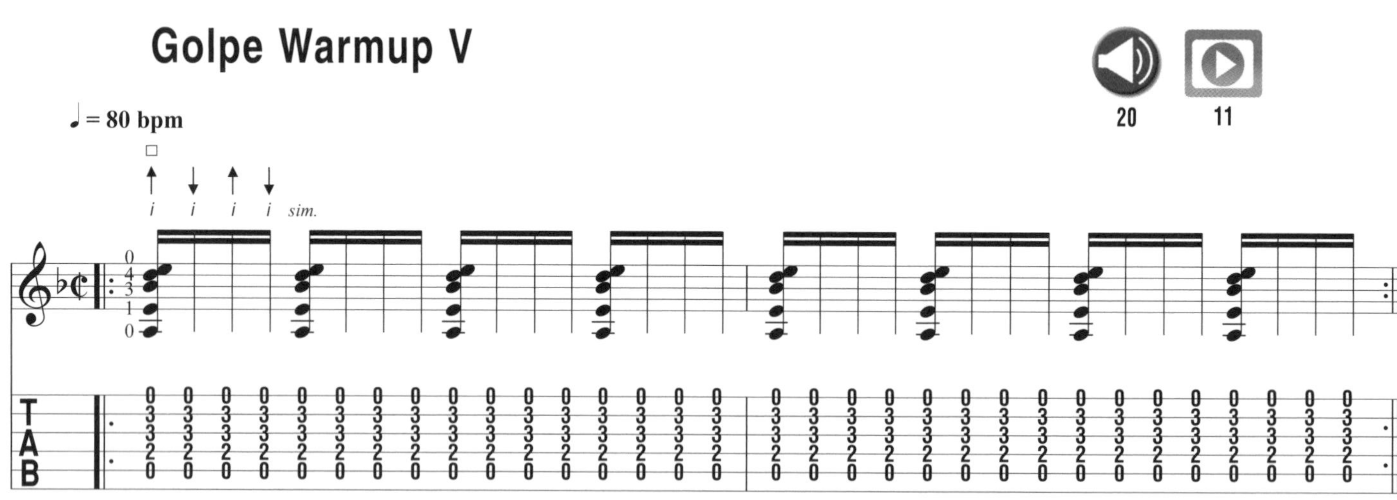

Golpe Warmup VI

21 12

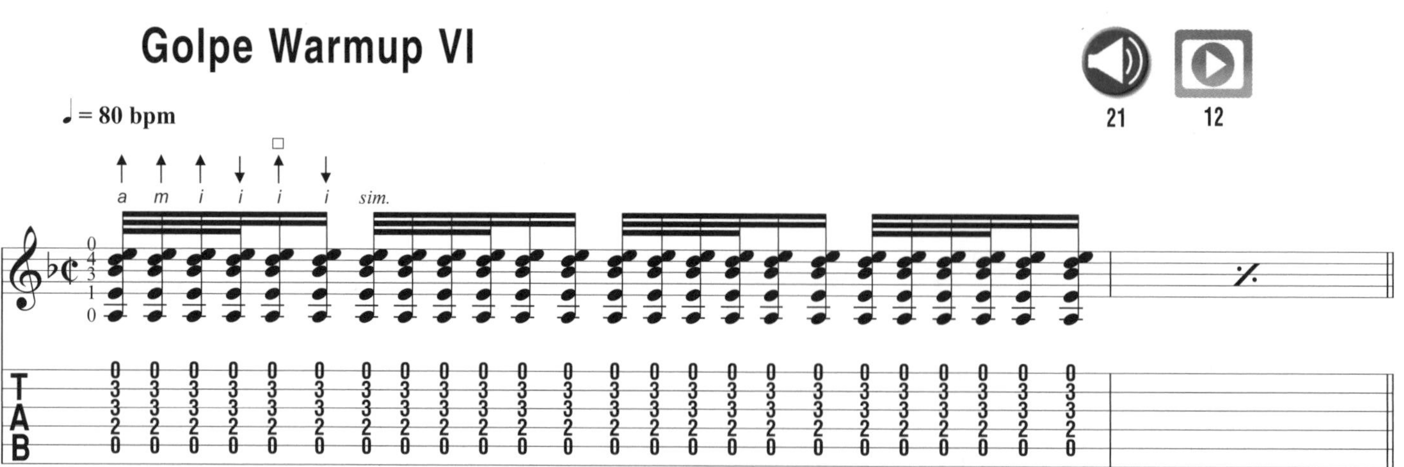

GOLPE PALO ETUDES

Tangos

22 13

♩ = 130 bpm

Bulerías

23 14

♩ = 110 bpm

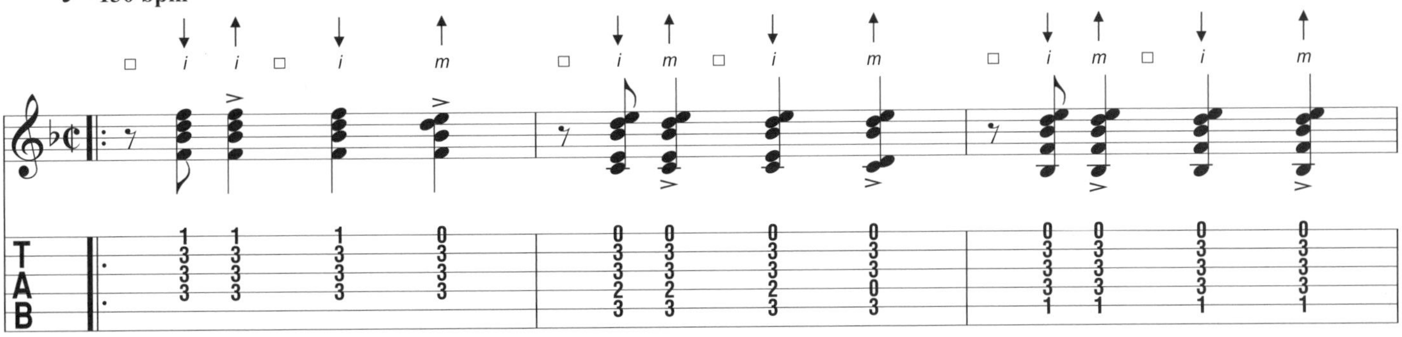

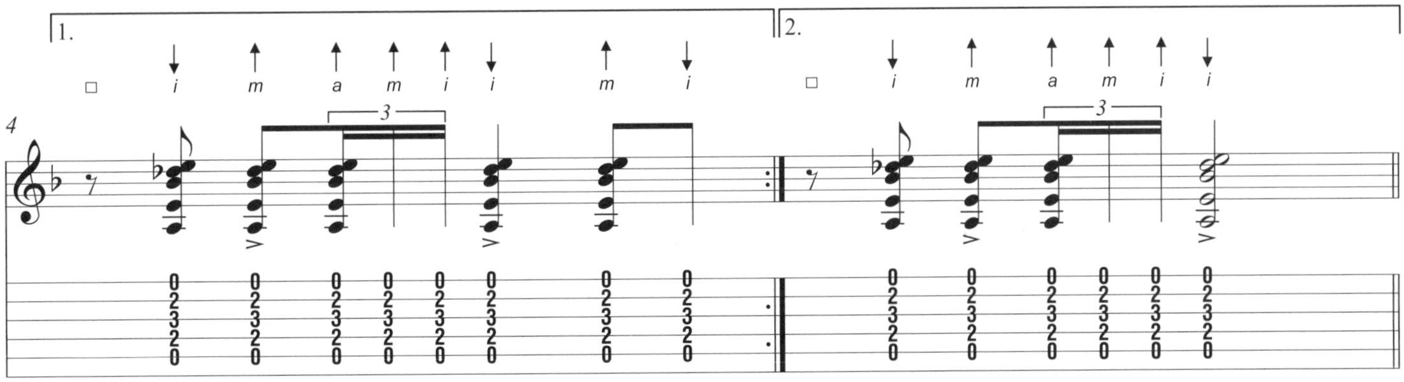

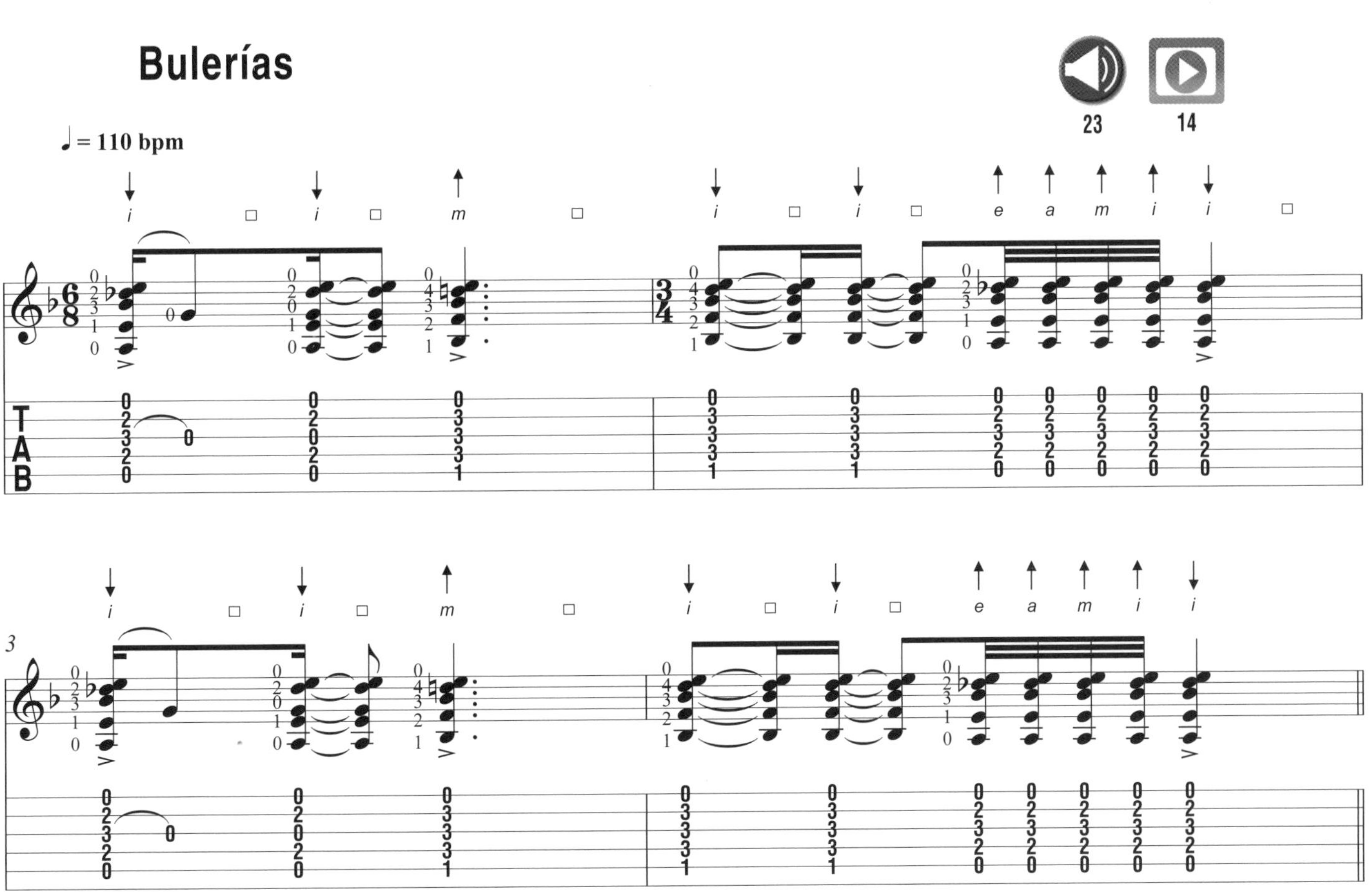

Alegrías

24 15

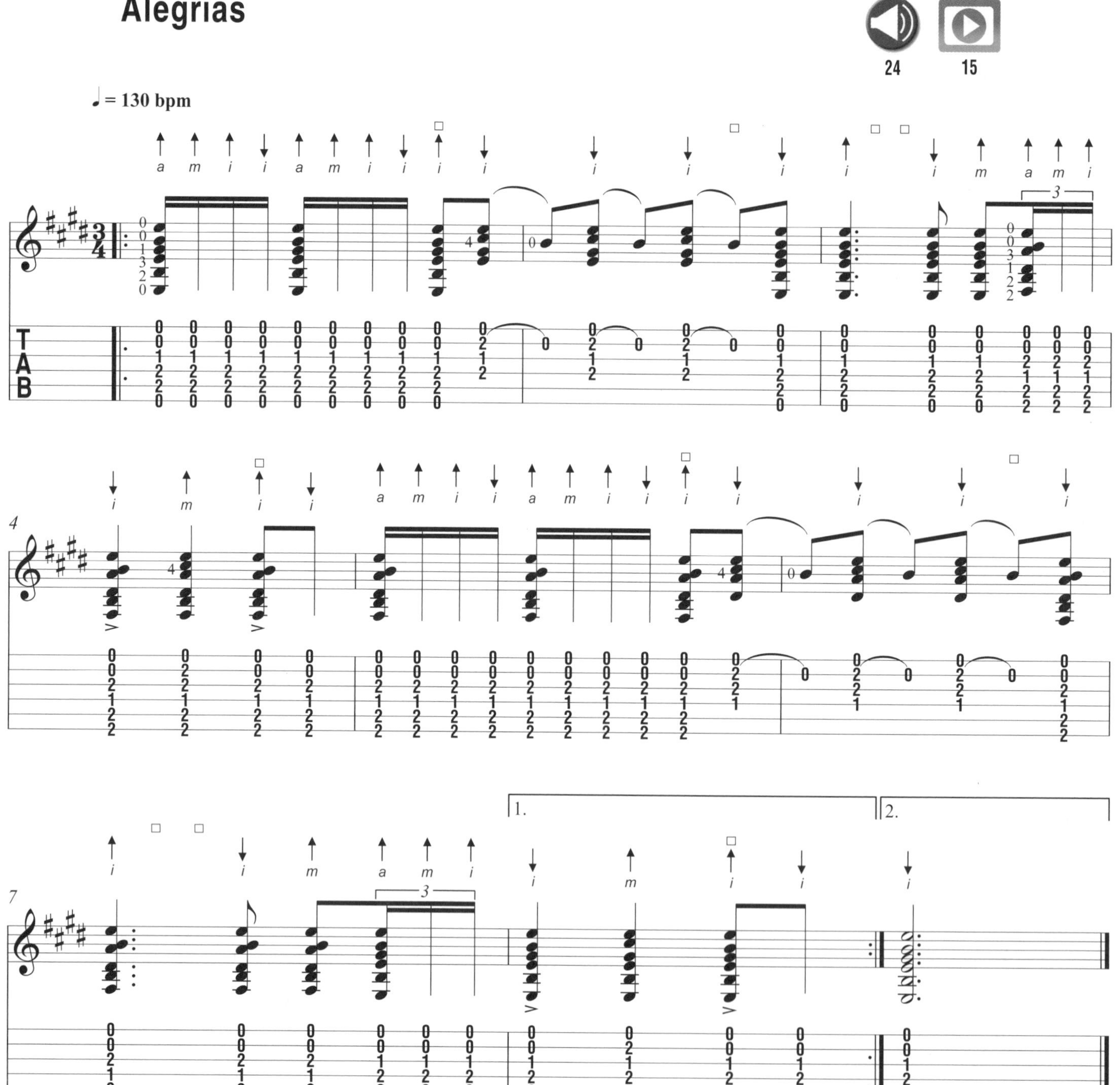

CHAPTER 6

Arpegio

FIG. 6.1. Hand Position for Arpegio

Arpegio (arpeggio) is the strumming-hand technique of playing a chord's notes in succession—one after the other.

Arpegio is a fundamental technique in flamenco guitar, also commonly occurring in classical guitar. It is essential to develop strong and balanced arpegios in order to play any palo successfully.

ARPEGIO WARMUP EXERCISES

We will begin by warming up with some exercises that isolate the different types of arpegios. Then, we will use them in a series of palo etudes.

First, adopt the correct position: fingers straight down (90 degrees to the strings), thumb pointing away from the fingers. This is the ideal beginning position; you can adapt it to your comfort.

The thumb only plays the lower strings (*bajos* or *bordones*): 6, 5, and 4. The fingers only play the upper strings (*primas*): 3, 2, and 1. The thumb should not intrude into the same area as where the other fingers play. After playing a note, your thumb should land to rest on the next string (*apoyando*, or "supporting"): 6 to 5, 5 to 4, and 4 back to 6. It should always have a resting point and never be away from the strings.

To play an even arpegio, slowly practice it with a metronome. Start by setting your metronome to 60 bpm and gradually increase the speed. Your goal should be to produce a balanced sound in all the notes of the arpegio rather than to play fast.

In flamenco guitar, we use the following types of arpegios:

1. **Upward Arpegio** (*Arpegio hacia arriba*). Strumming-hand fingering is *p a m i*.

CIII
1.
CI

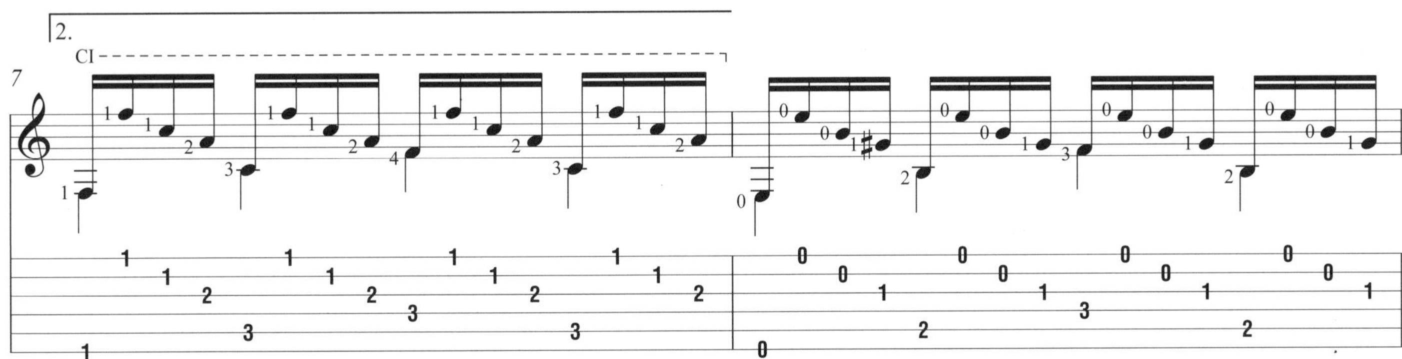
2.
CI

2. **Backward Arpegio** (*Arpegio hacia abajo*). Strumming-hand fingering is *p i m a*.

♩ = 100 bpm

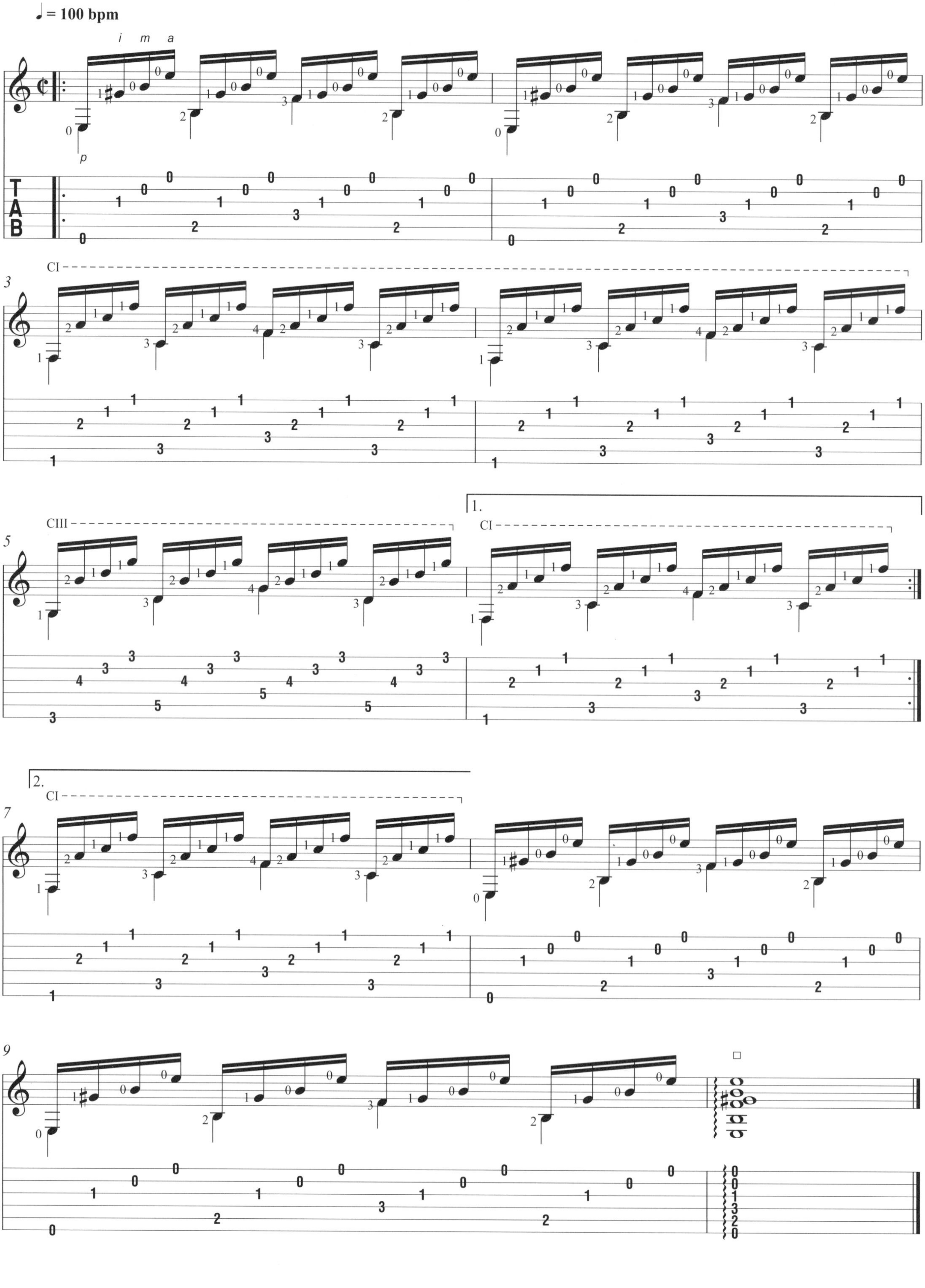

3. **Double Arpegio** (*Arpegio doble*). Strumming-hand fingering is *p i m a m i.*

♩ = 100 bpm

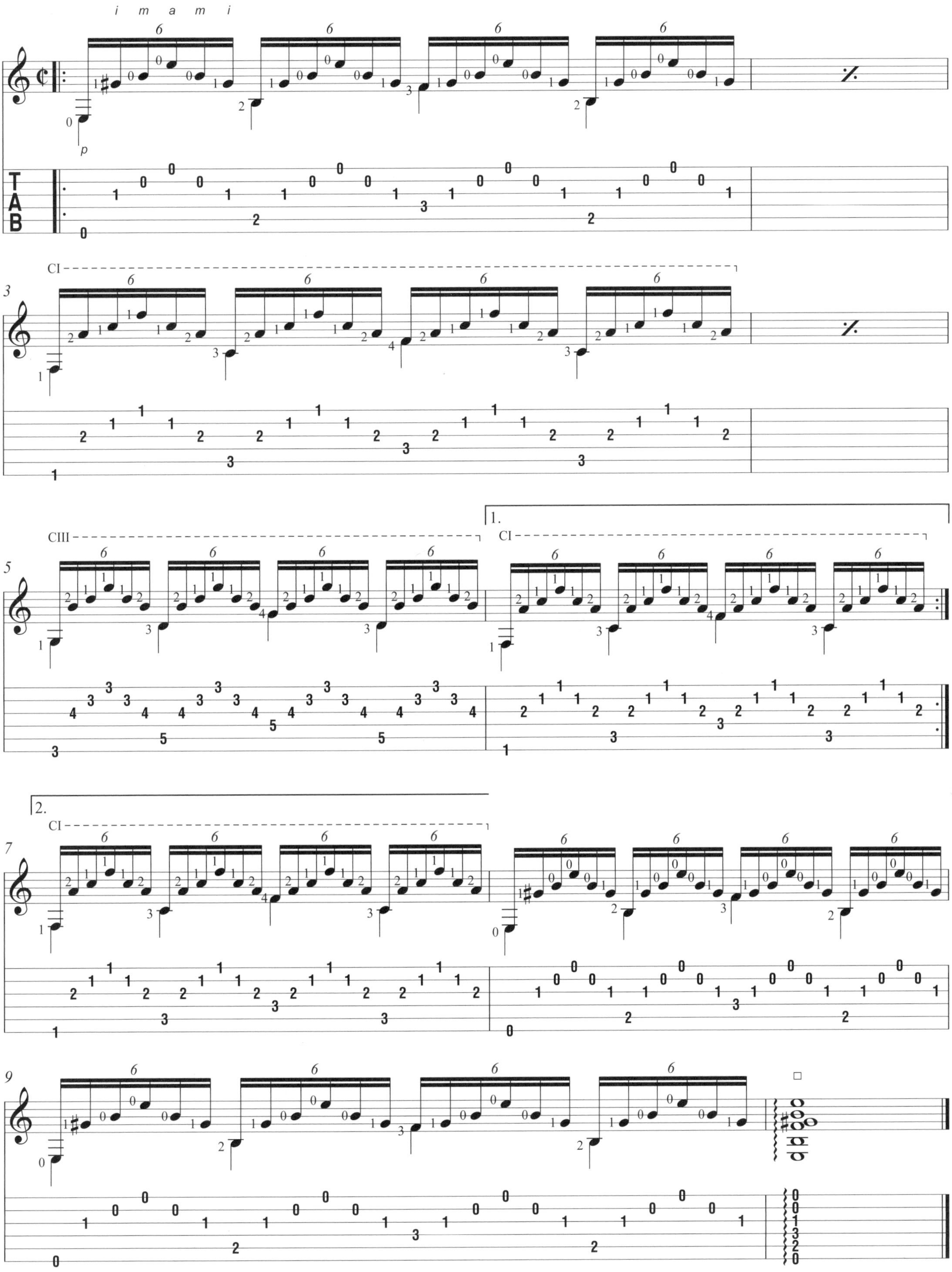

4. Middle Arpegio (*Arpegio medio*). Strumming-hand fingering is *p m i a*.

♩ = 100 bpm

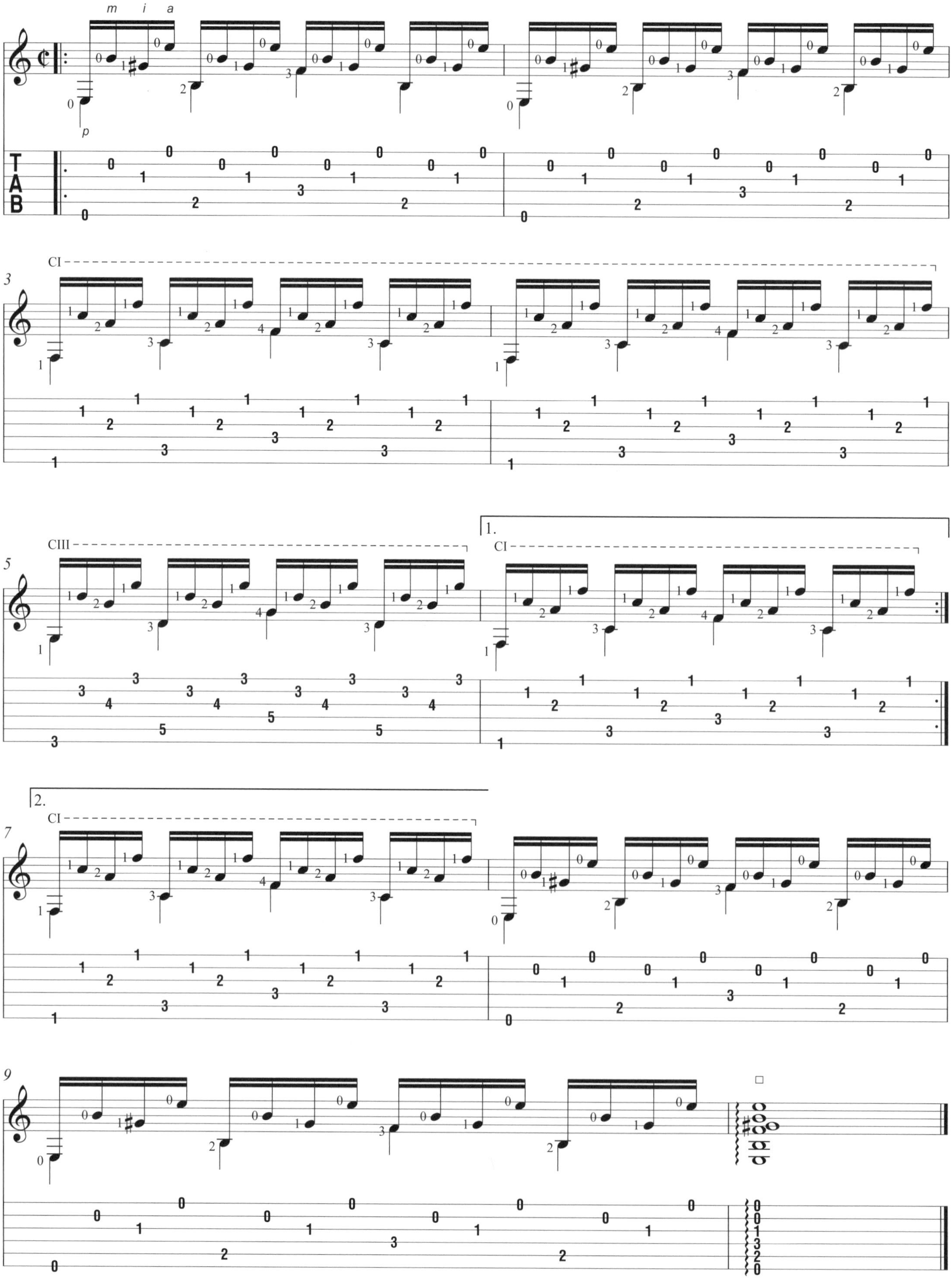

5. Middle Double Arpegio (*Arpegio medio doble*). Strumming-hand fingering is *p m i a m i*.

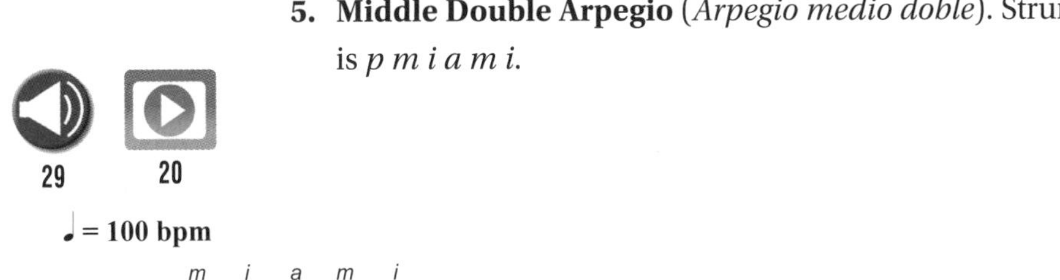

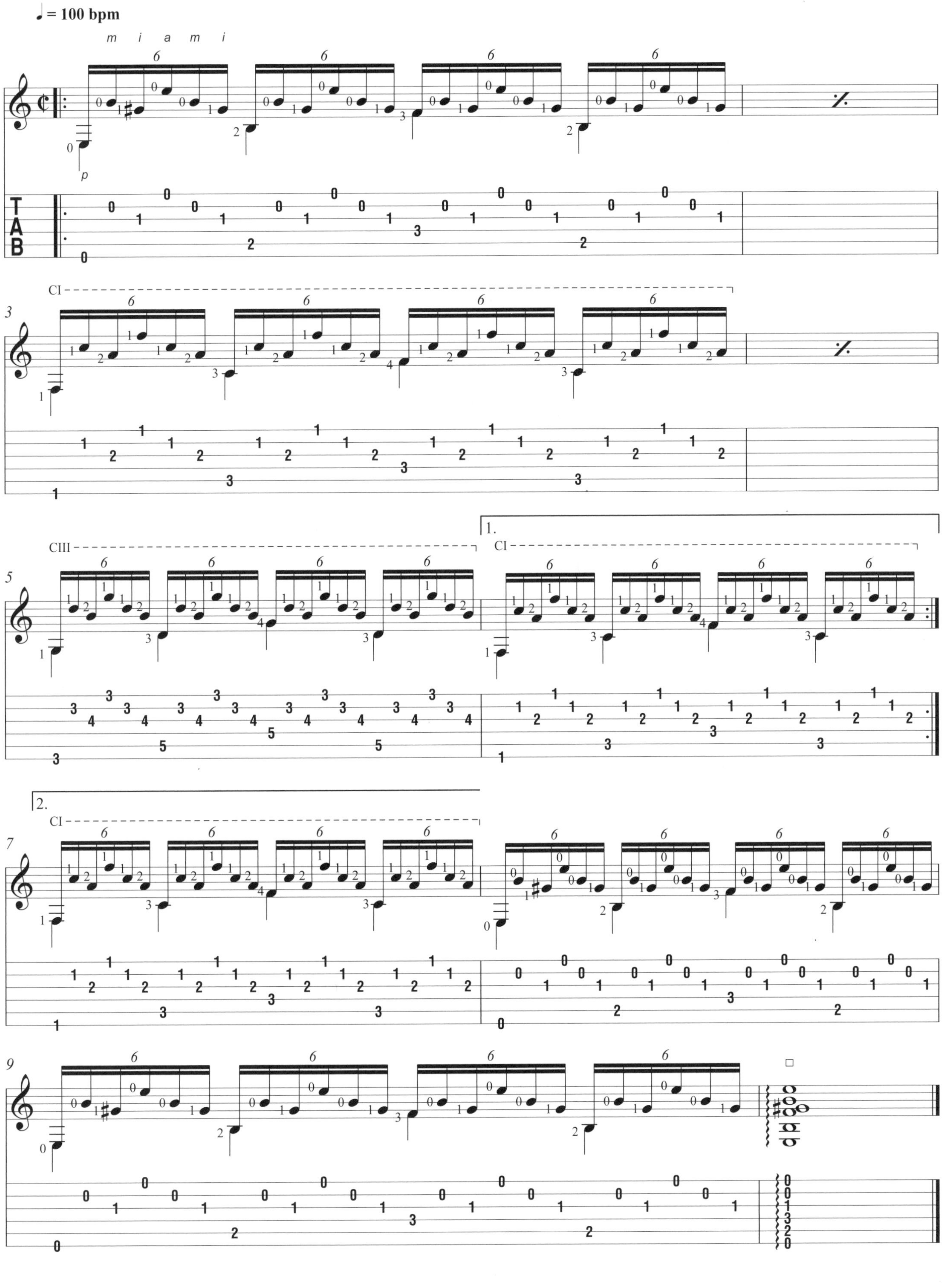

ARPEGIO PALO ETUDES

Soleá

30 21

♩ = 100 bpm

Soleá por Bulerías

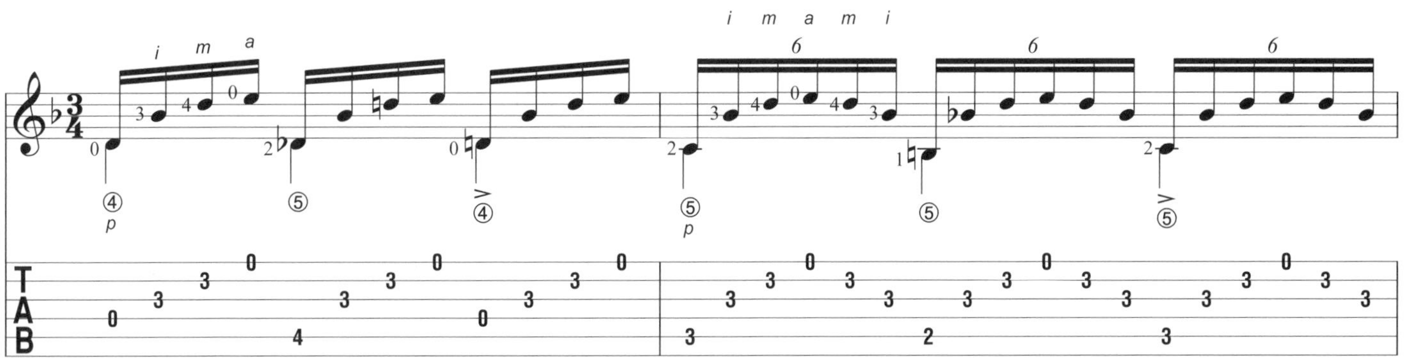

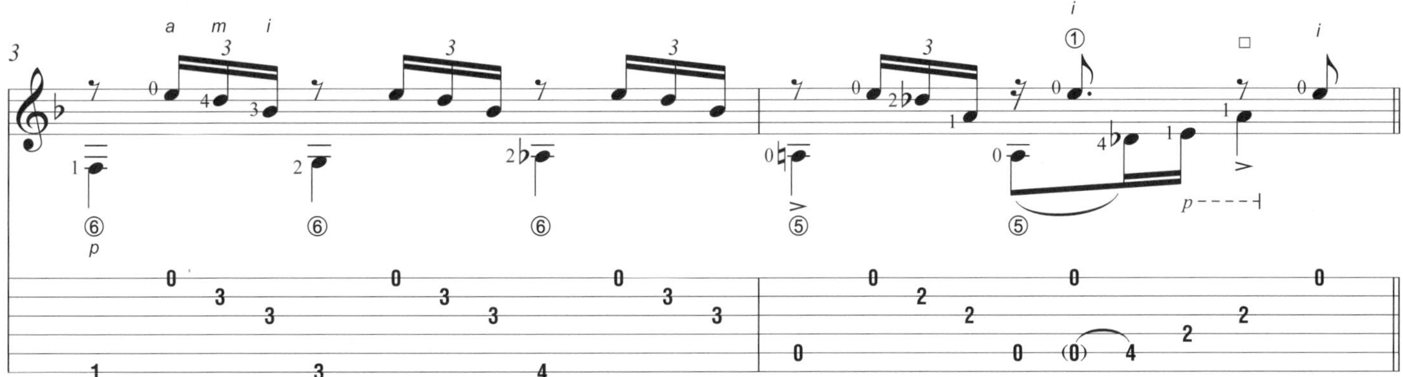

Alegrías

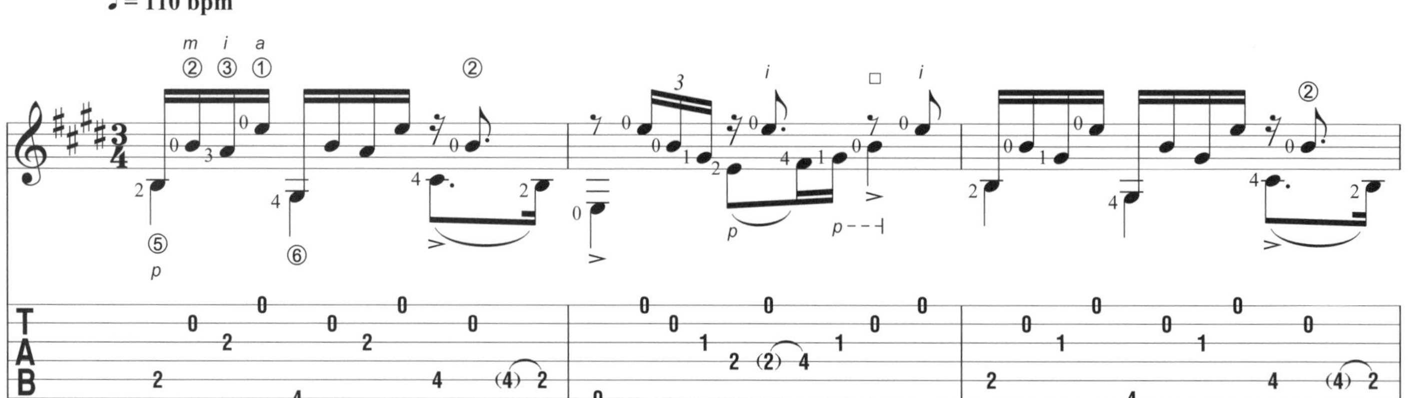

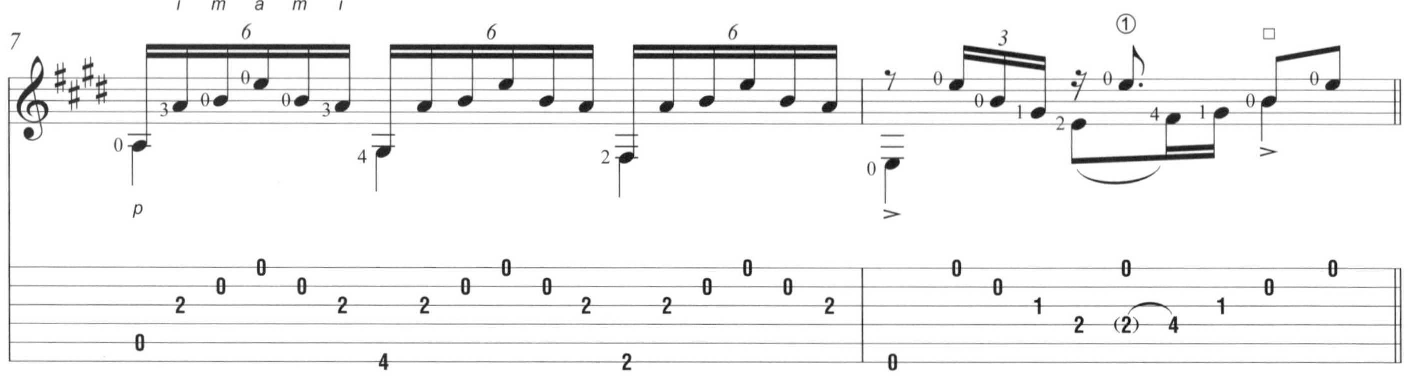

CHAPTER 7

Pulgar

FIG. 7.1. Thumb Position for Pulgar

Pulgar is the Spanish word for "thumb." The pulgar (thumb) technique is used to strike strings in sequence, achieving a series of individually struck notes that can be interwoven with any number of ligados (see lesson 11). The movement comes from the wrist, and when developed properly, can produce great effects.

In order to execute the pulgar technique correctly, keep your thumb straight but relaxed, and attack the strings by slightly rotating your wrist. Once you play a note, rest your thumb on the next string (apoyando). As a functional study of the technique itself, point your thumb up, straight (like the "okay" sign), and then rotate your wrist so that your thumb points down. Keep your other fingers relaxed. Rotate your wrist to point your thumb down, up, down, up, etc., in order to get used to the technique. Then integrate that movement into your playing.

The movement must be relaxed, and the string should be attacked half and half with your nail and the fleshy part of your thumb. This way, we will incorporate the percussive and brighter element of the nail and the softness of the finger. This generates that crisp, full, percussive flamenco sound.

While familiarizing yourself with the pulgar technique, try tucking your index finger underneath your thumb, as if holding a pick, and practice short scale passages, as well as the following warmup exercises.

PULGAR WARMUP EXERCISES

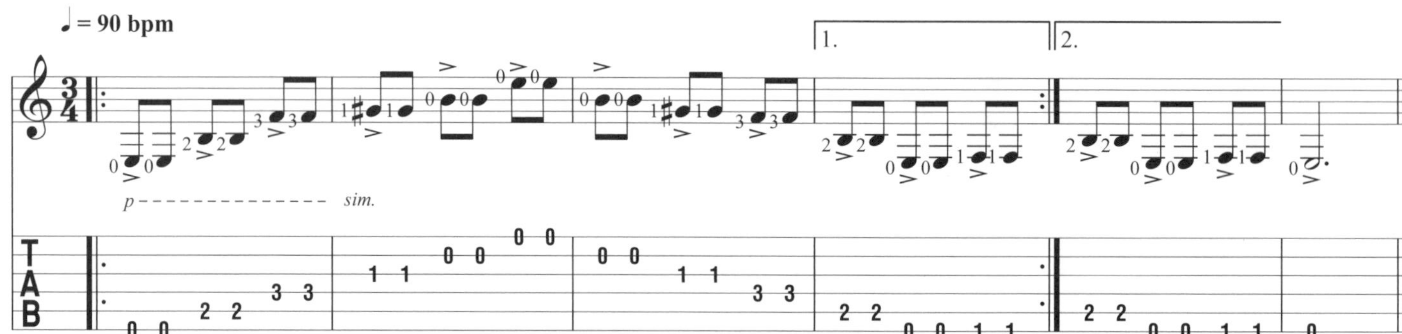

Pulgar Warmup II

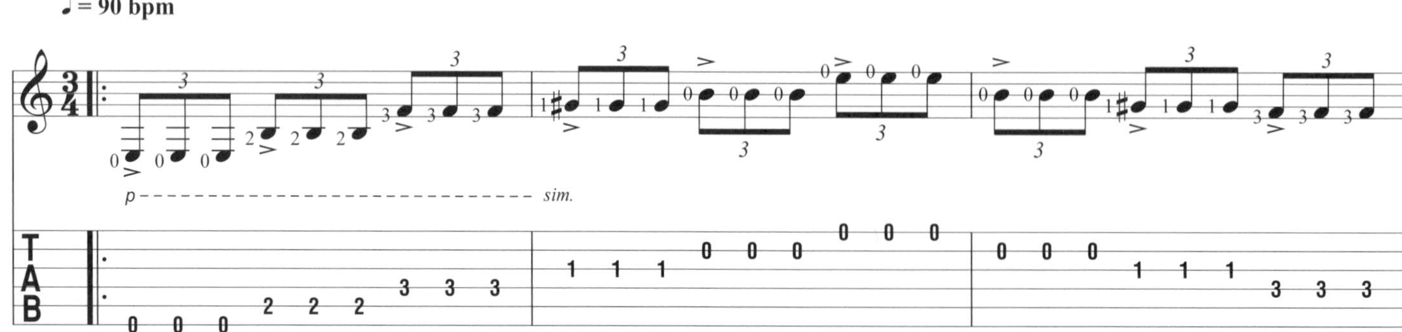

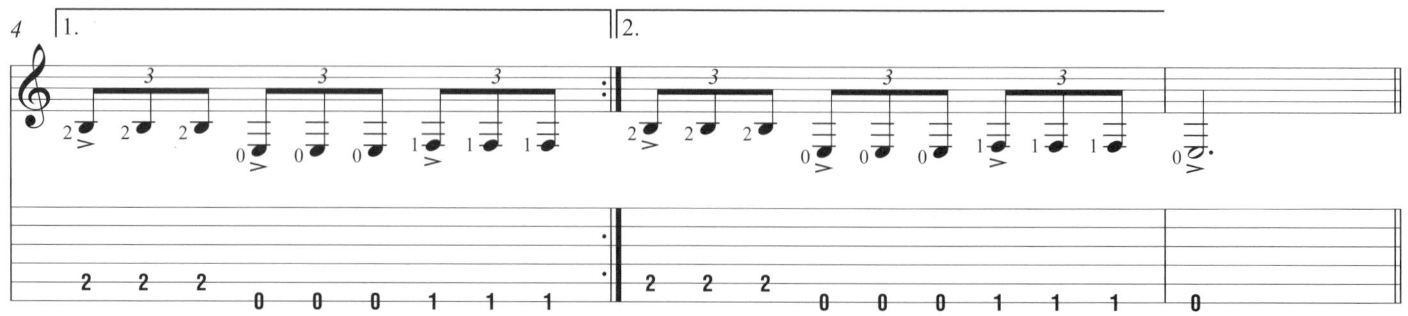

Pulgar Warmup III

♩ = 90 bpm

PULGAR PALO ETUDES

Alegrías

36 27

Soleá

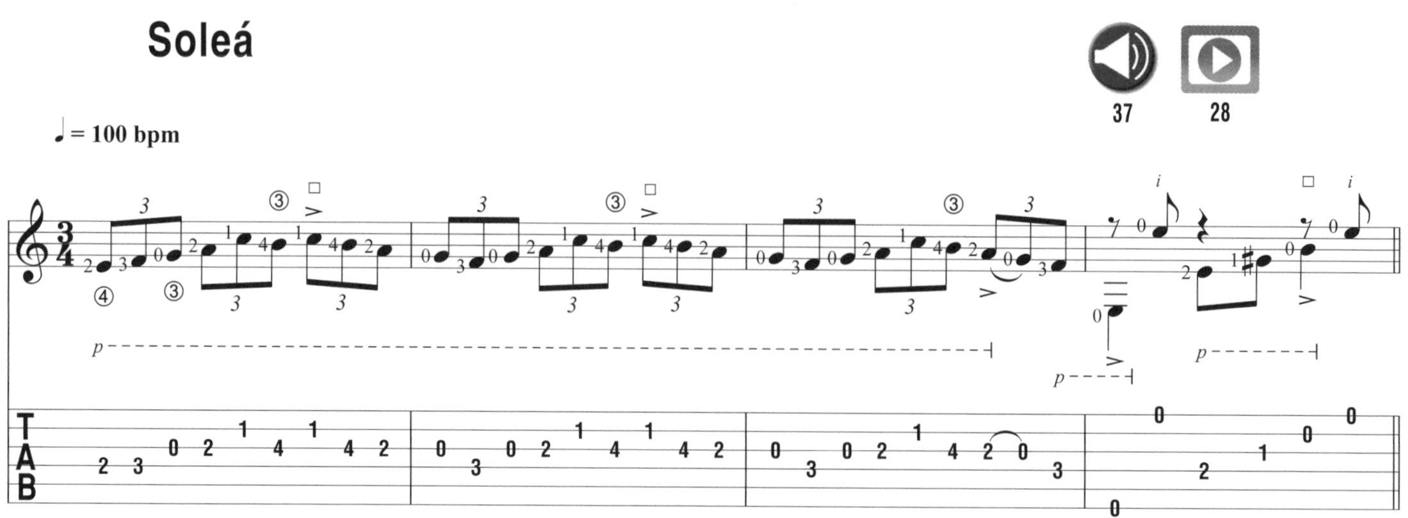

Bulerías

CHAPTER 8

Picado

FIG. 8.1. Picado Hand Position

Picado, which literally means "chopped," is a two-finger stroke that is performed by alternating the index and middle fingers. Attack the strings with a combination of the nail and the finger, half and half, as in pulgar technique. Keep your fingers straight, and move from your large, first knuckle, which is where the strength of this attack comes from. After playing a string, rest your finger on the adjacent string (apoyando, as with the thumb).

Alternate picado methods include using the index and ring finger, or even middle and ring finger. As soon as a finger plays a note, the previous finger replaces the other finger. Do not repeat the same finger on a string.

The force of the movement comes from the knuckle rather than from the articulation of the finger.

PICADO WARMUP EXERCISES

Continue these fingering patterns through all strings, first from the high to low string, and then from the low to the high string.

Picado Warmup I

39 30

♩ = 100 bpm

Picado Warmup II

40 31

♩ = 100 bpm

Picado Warmup III

41 32

♩ = 100 bpm

PICADO PALO ETUDES

Soleá

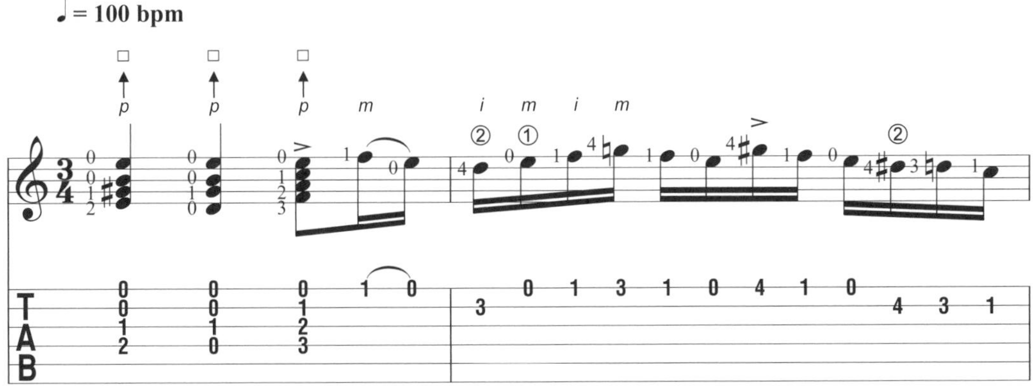

Guajira

43 34

Bulerías

44 35

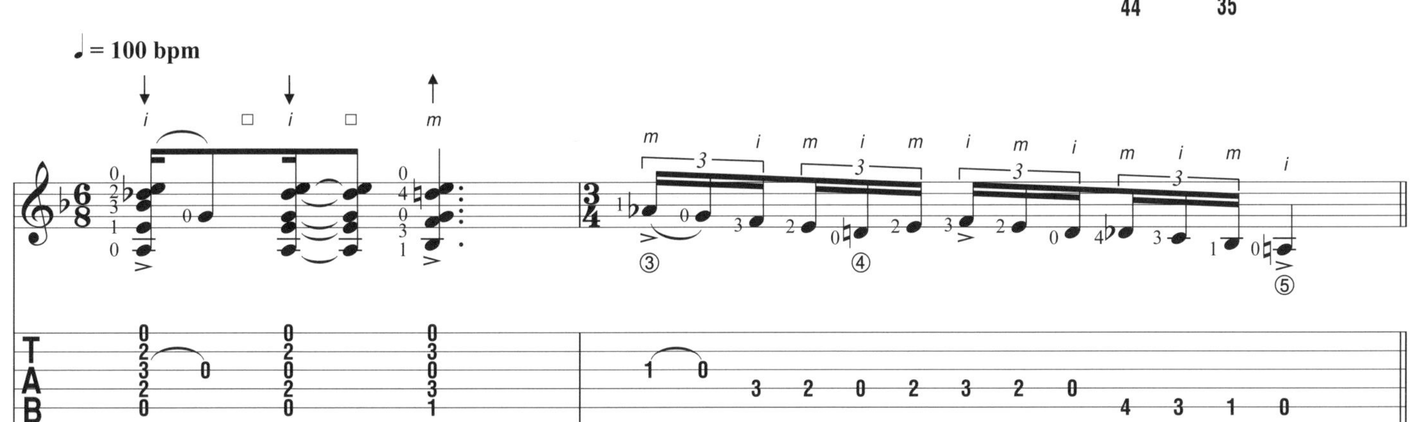

Fandango de Huelva

45 36

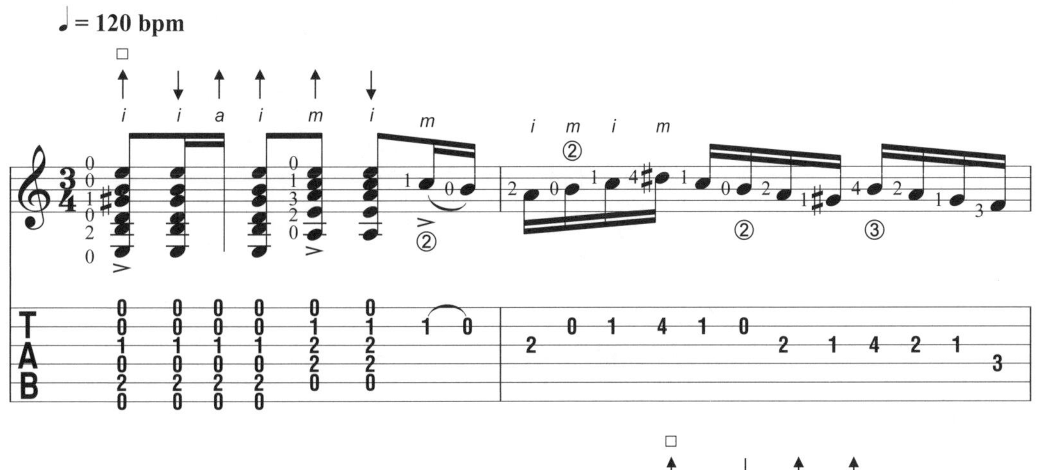

CHAPTER 9

Alzapúa

FIG. 9.1. Alzapúa Hand Position

Alzapúa technique is an important and characteristic aspect of the flamenco guitar, and it is hardly ever played in any other guitar music. The term alzapúa comes from the Spanish verb *"alzar,"* meaning "to lift" or "to raise," and the term *"púa,"* which directly translates into "plectrum." In this technique, the thumb acts like a plectrum.

This technique employs thumb upstrokes and downstrokes, generally in triplets or sixteenth notes. These are the three main movements involved.

1. In the first stroke, the thumb plays the bass note (normally placed on the fourth, fifth, or sixth string of the guitar), using a downstroke, and resting on the next string (apoyando).
2. The second stroke is a downward movement in which the thumb plays two or three strings. Usually, this second stroke is performed with a hit (*golpe,* see lesson 5) on the tap plate with the middle finger.

3. In the third stroke, the thumb goes upward, playing the same strings as the second stroke. They are articulated with the nail only.

Practice alzapúa technique in triplets. Place your hand close to the guitar bridge, a bit further than halfway between the guitar sound hole and the bridge.

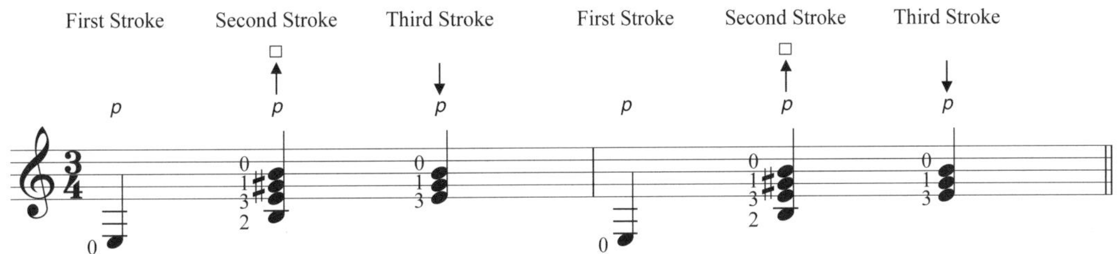

FIG. 9.2. Alzapúa Three Strokes

ALZAPÚA WARMUP EXERCISES

Alzapúa Warmup I

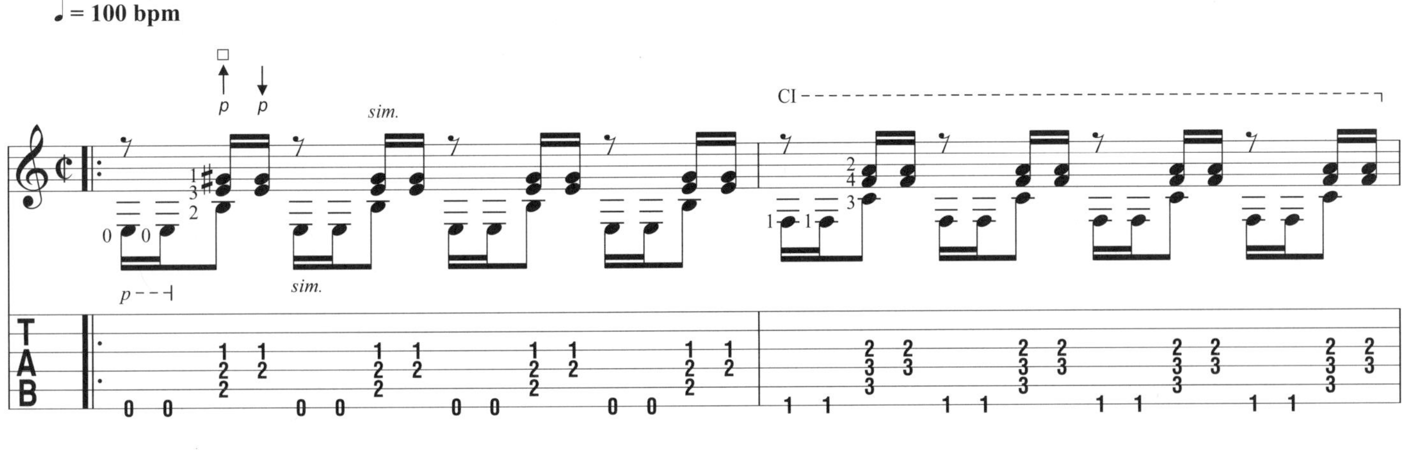

Alzapúa Warmup II

Alzapúa Warmup III

ALZAPÚA PALO ETUDES

Tangos

49 40

♩ = 130 bpm

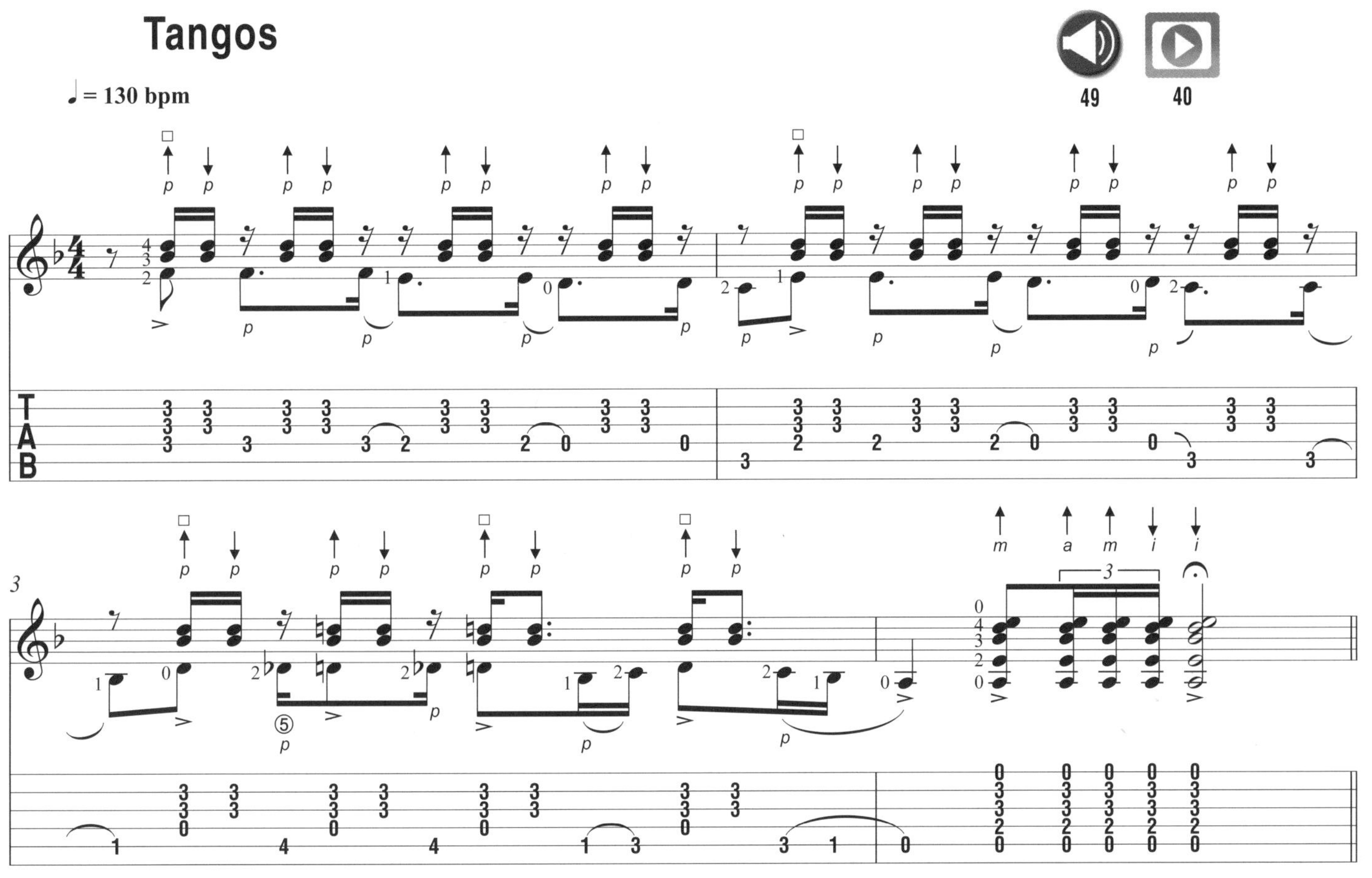

Bulerías

50 41

♩ = 110 bpm

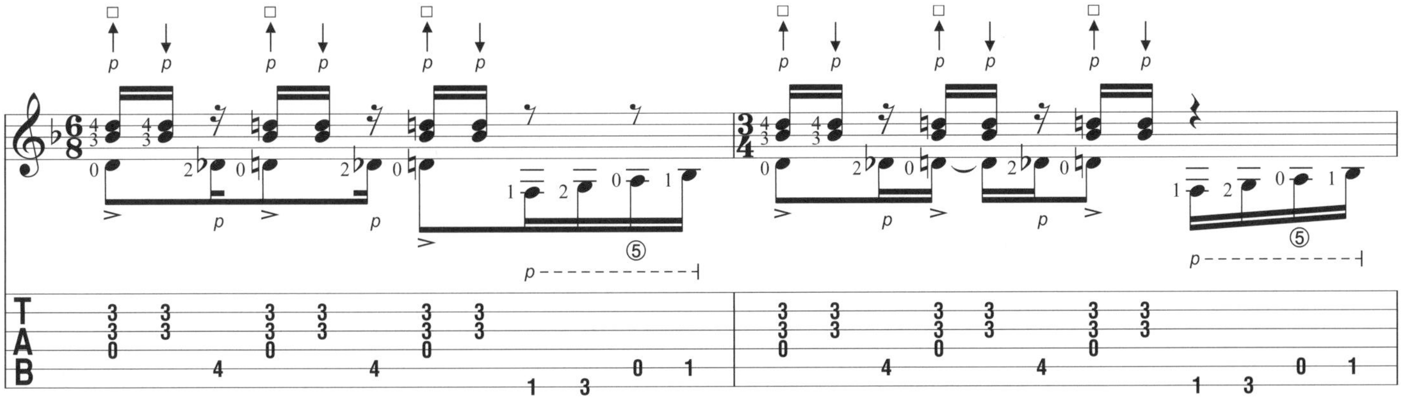

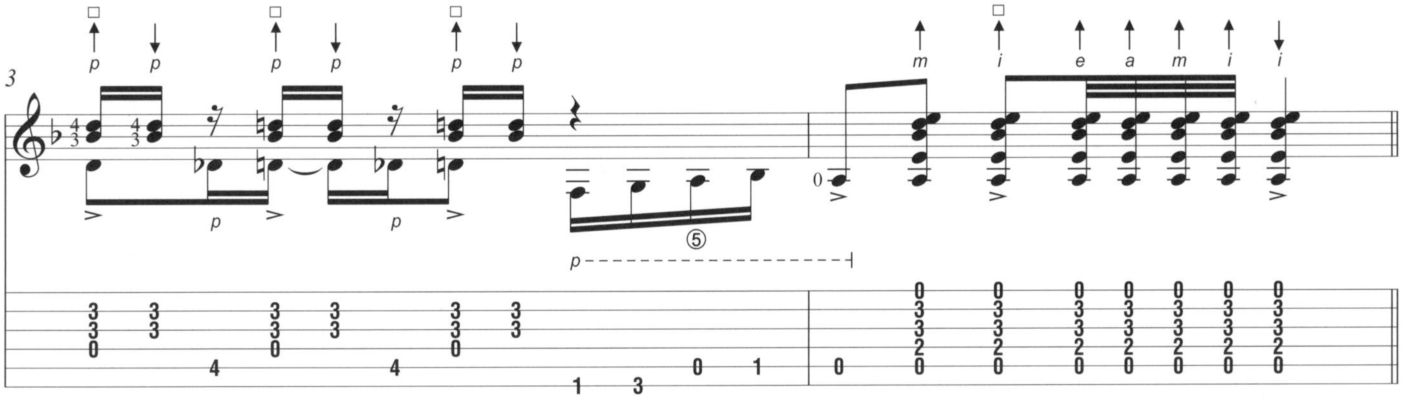

Fandango de Huelva

51 42

♩ = 130 bpm

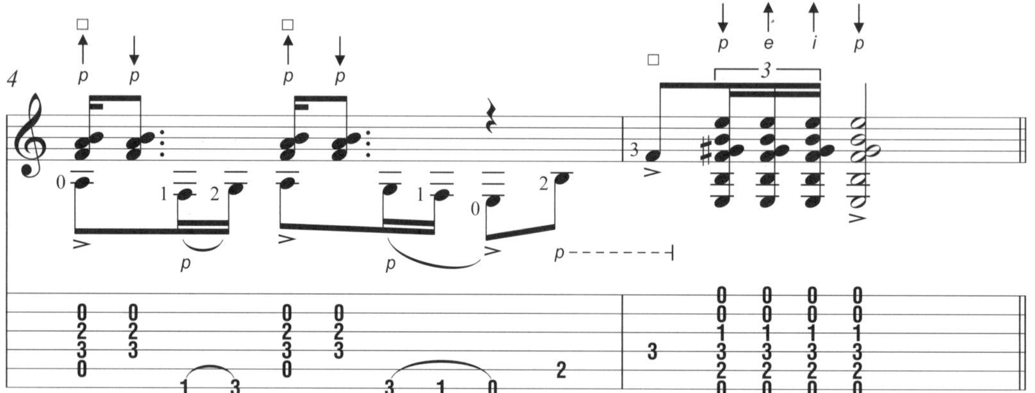

CHAPTER 10

Pulgar/Índice

FIG. 10.1. Pulgar/Índice Hand Position

Pulgar/Índice (thumb/index) technique refers to playing with the thumb in the lower strings (*bajos* or *bordones*) and the index in the upper strings (*primas*). The first note is played with the thumb; the index finger completes the figure.

We can either play the two notes simultaneously or sequentially. This technique is broadly used in all flamenco palos, and along with rajeo (or *rasgueado*), it is one of the most characteristic techniques in flamenco music.

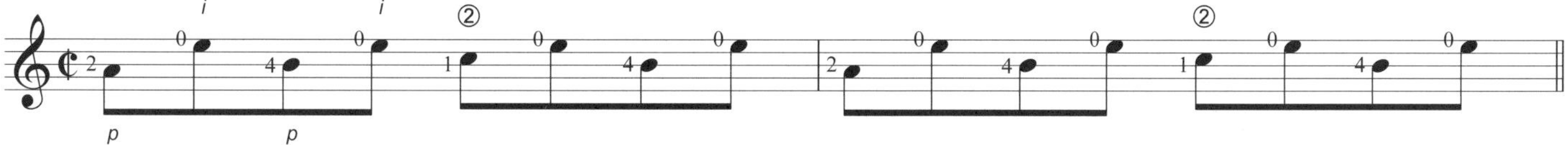

FIG. 10.2. Pulgar/Índice Figure

PULGAR/ÍNDICE WARMUP EXERCISES

Pulgar/Índice Warmup I

52 43

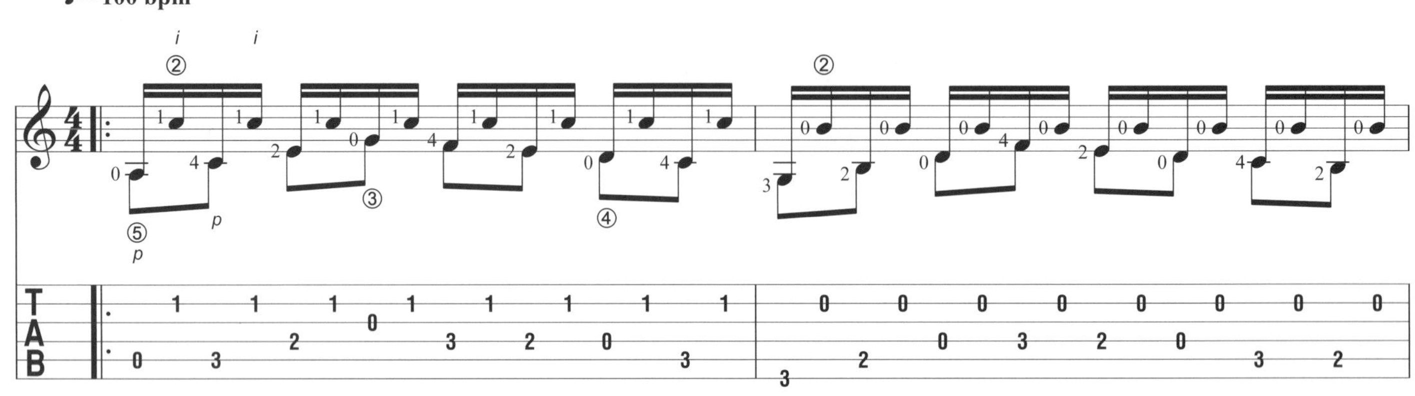

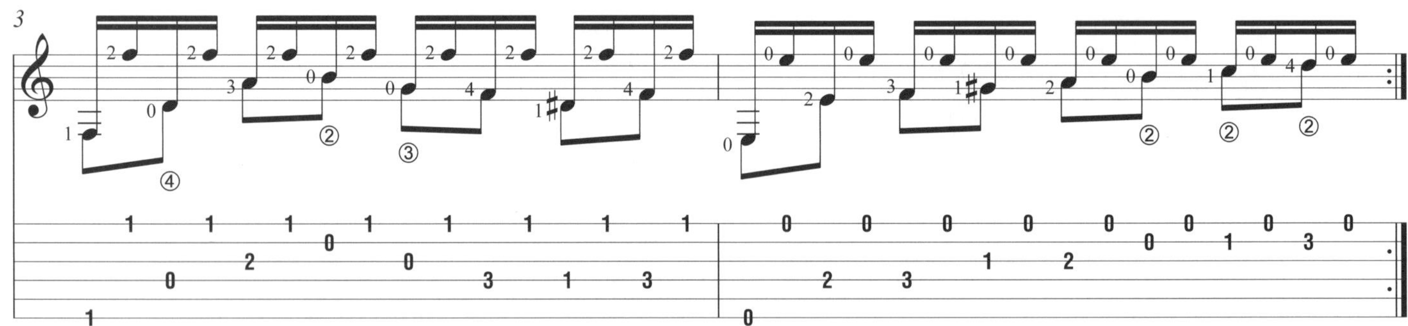

Pulgar/Índice Warmup II

53 44

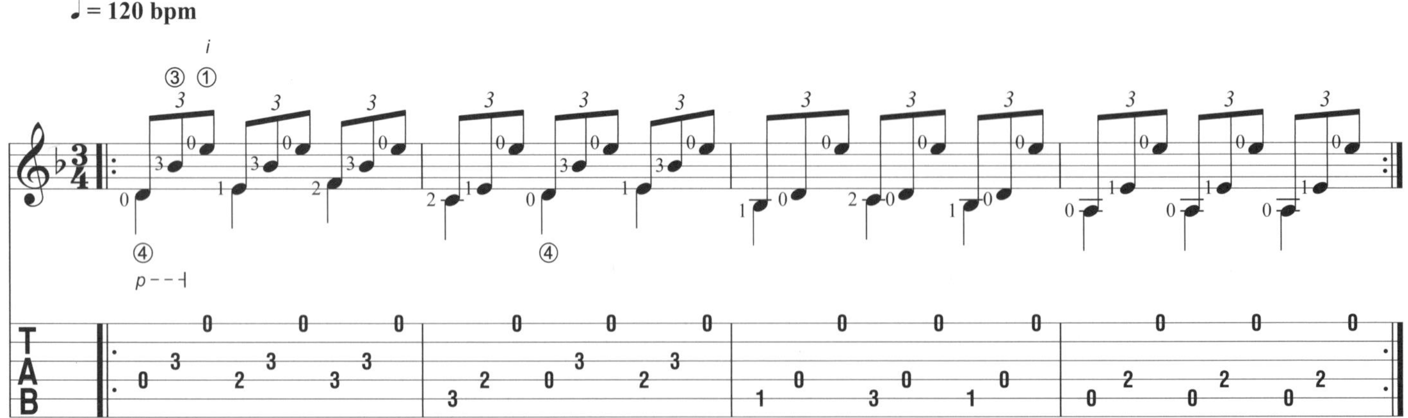

PULGAR/ÍNDICE PALO ETUDES

Soleá

54 45

♩= 100 bpm

Bulerías

55 46

♩= 100 bpm

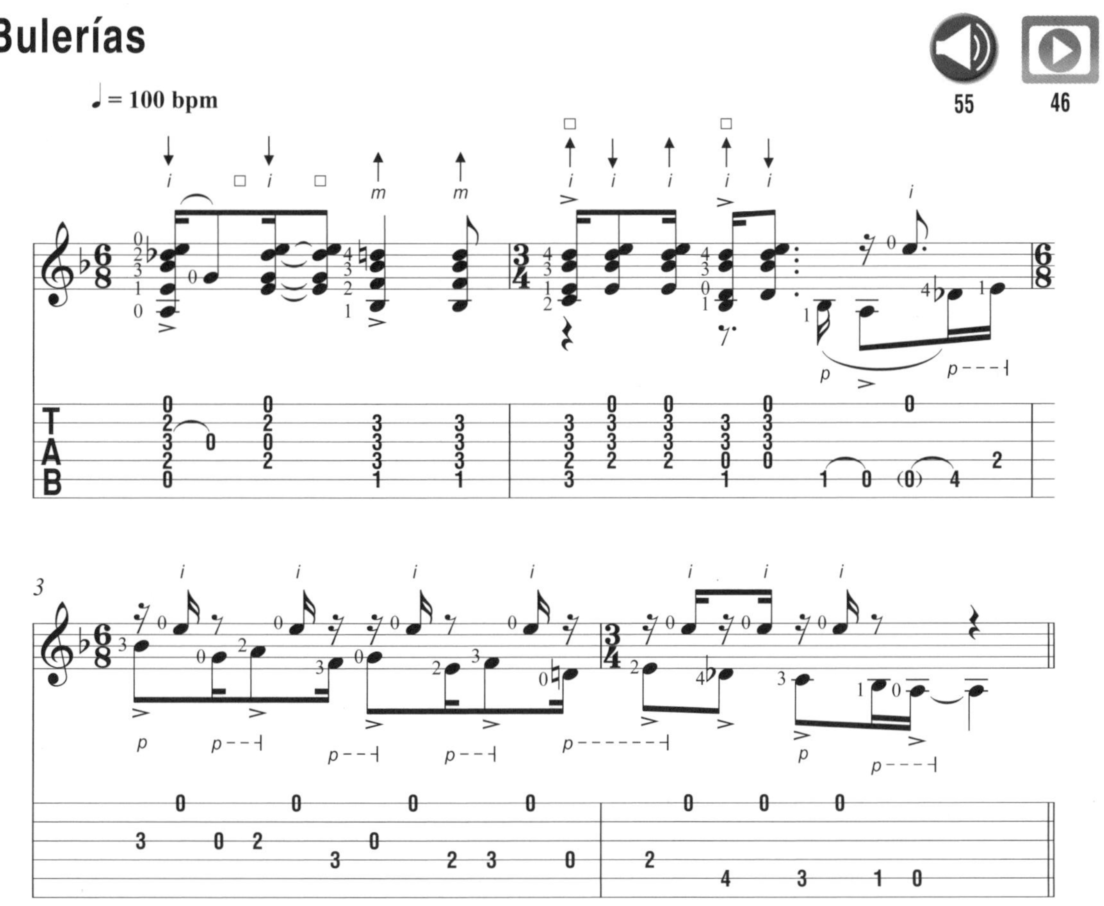

CHAPTER 11

Ligado

Ligado (slur) is a fretboard-hand technique that consists of either hammering a finger down or pulling it off of a string, causing it to sound a second note after it is initially plucked. Ligado is indicated by a slur above or beneath the notes to be played (see figure 11.1)

At first, the strumming hand plays a note, and the fretboard-hand finger(s) either hammers on (*ascending ligado*) or pulls off (*descending ligado*) the same string, producing another note. Flamenco players use this technique to create fast note runs, most of the time plucking the string with the pulgar technique, but also possibly with picado technique. Ligado can be employed by any fretboard-hand finger, causing a rapid, slurring effect.

Ligado technique helps you to gain agility and speed in your fretboard hand. At first, practice them slowly, trying to have the same sound intensity on both plucked note with the strumming hand and the ligado note sounded by the fretboard hand.

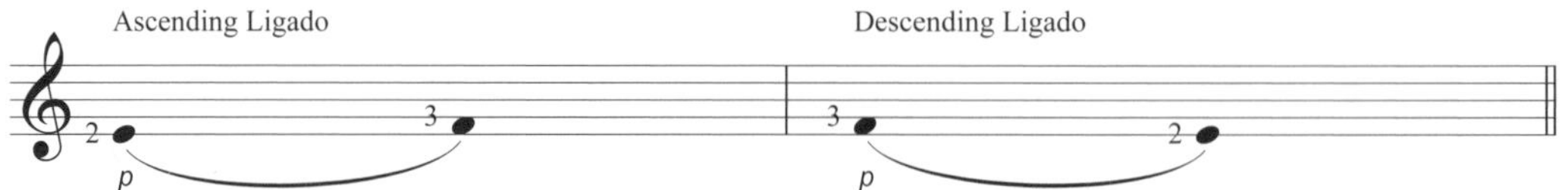

FIG. 11.1. Ligado Ascending and Descending

LIGADO WARMUP EXERCISE

Practice ligado in the following two ways:

1. Use the thumb to initially sound the string.
2. Use the middle and index fingers (picado) to initially sound the string.

Continue this exercise on all strings, first from low to high and then back down from high to low. Practice it by initially plucking the string with the thumb and with the index/middle fingers.

LIGADO PALO ETUDES

Guajira

57 48

♩ = 100 bpm

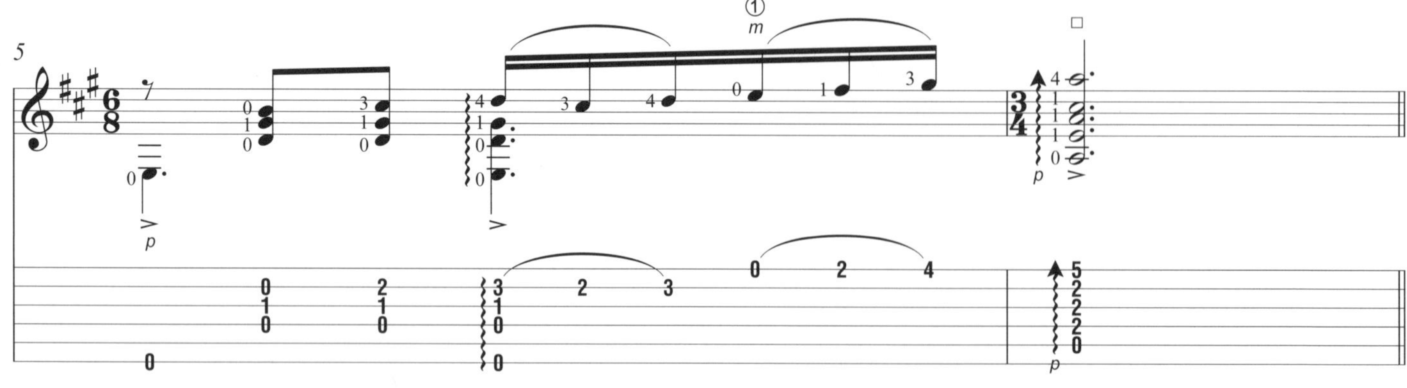

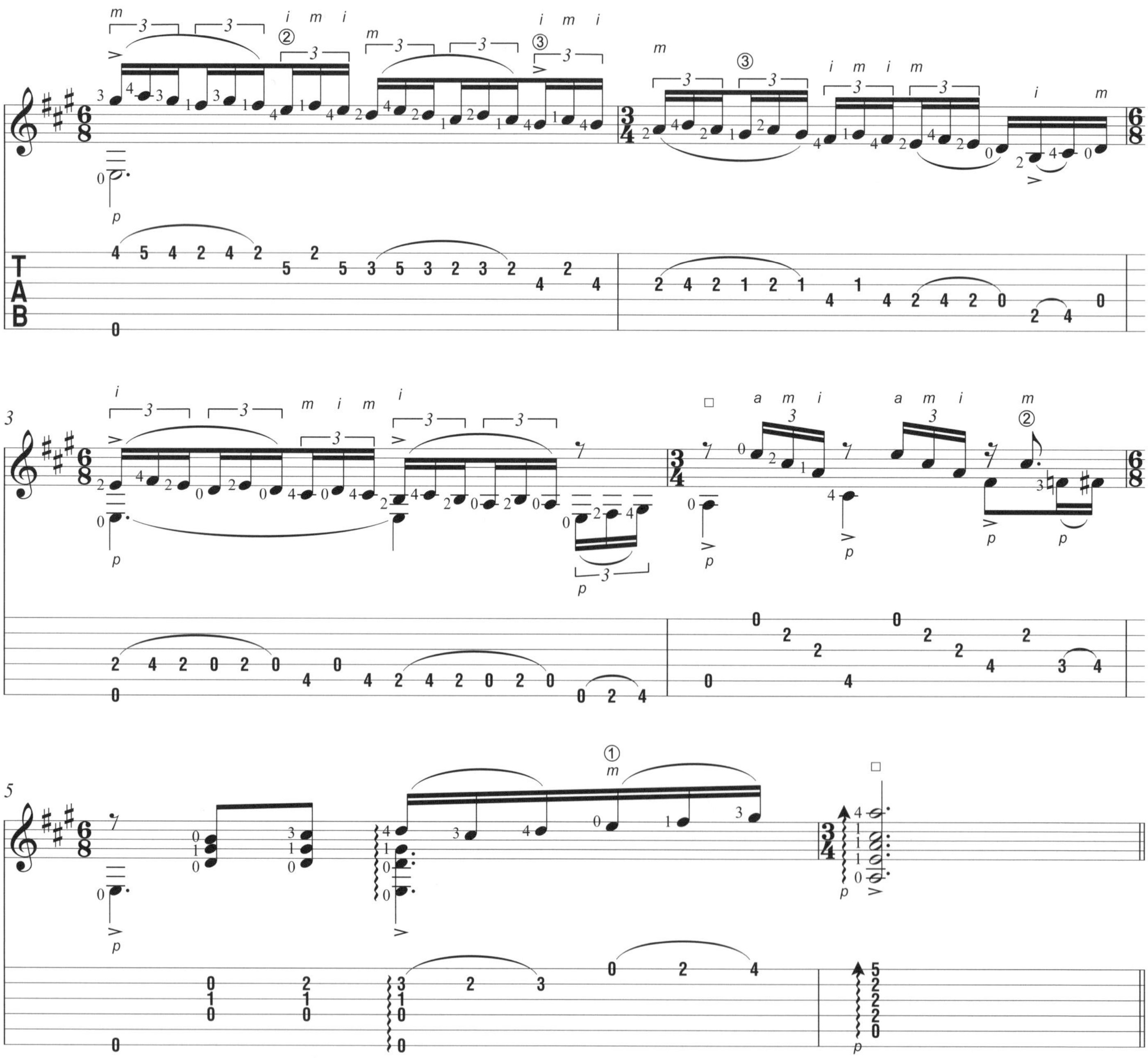

Bulerías

♩= 110 bpm

58 49

Soleá

♩= 100 bpm

59 50

CHAPTER 12

Rajeo

FIG. 12.1. Rajeo Hand Position

Rajeo (or *rasgueado*) technique is a percussive element that flamenco guitarists use a lot. It consists of flicking the fingers (and thumb) across the strings, up or down, either individually or in fast succession. By using more fingers, you can play quarter notes, eighth notes, triplets, or sixteenth notes.

It is a challenging technique at the beginning, so practice rajeos slowly, and always with a metronome. Start practicing quarter notes using only the index finger playing an upstroke. Then, add the downstroke. Once you master the basic technique, you can also add the golpe with the ring finger in each stroke (see lesson 14).

When you can play quarter notes, you can practice triplets, eighth notes, and sixteenth notes, adding more fingers to your rajeos.

Rajeos are crucial when playing with a dancer, because they help us to imitate the rhythmic figurations that the dancers perform with the feet. It is important to always keep the time.

RAJEO WARMUP EXERCISES

Rajeo Warmup I: Quarter Notes

60

51

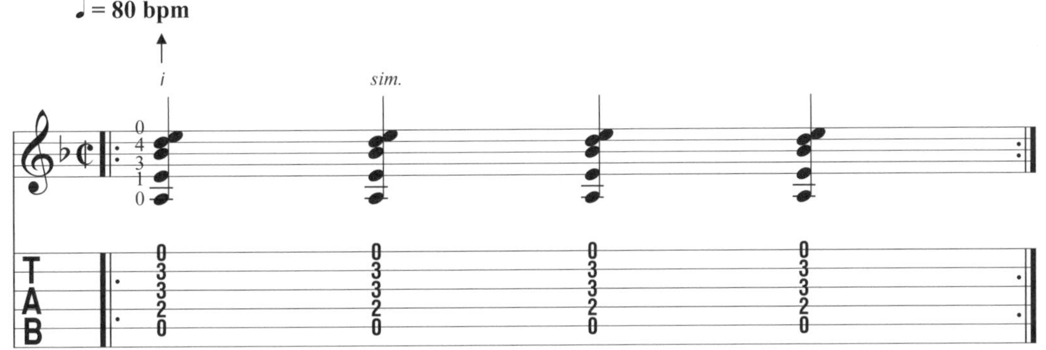

Rajeo Warmup II: Eighth Notes

61

52

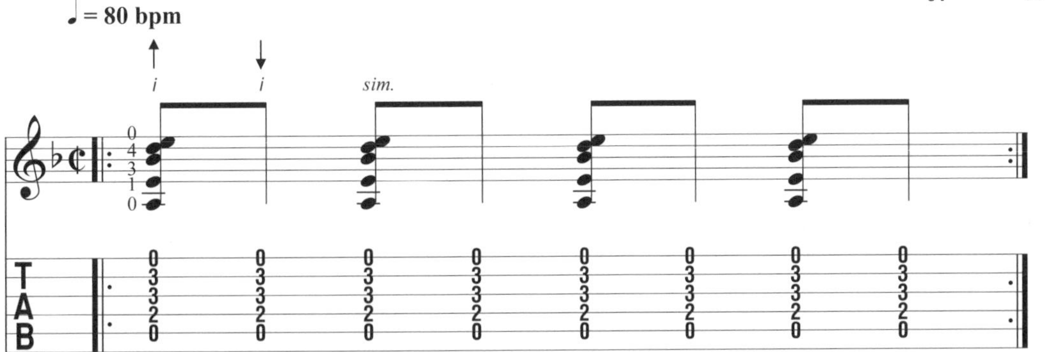

Rajeo Warmup III: Eighth Notes

62

53

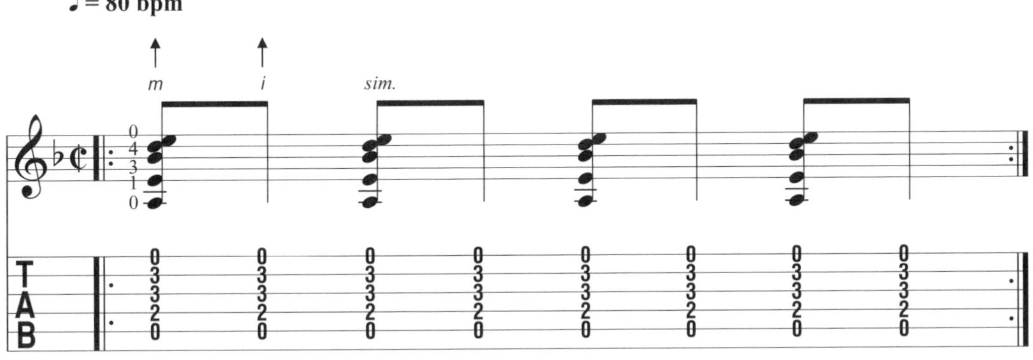

Rajeo Warmup IV: Triplets 1

63 54

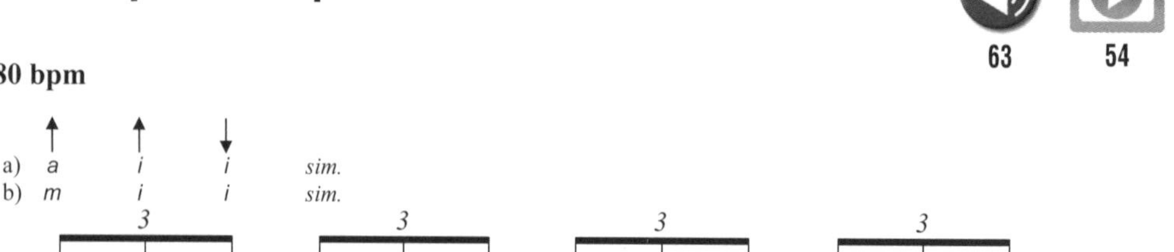

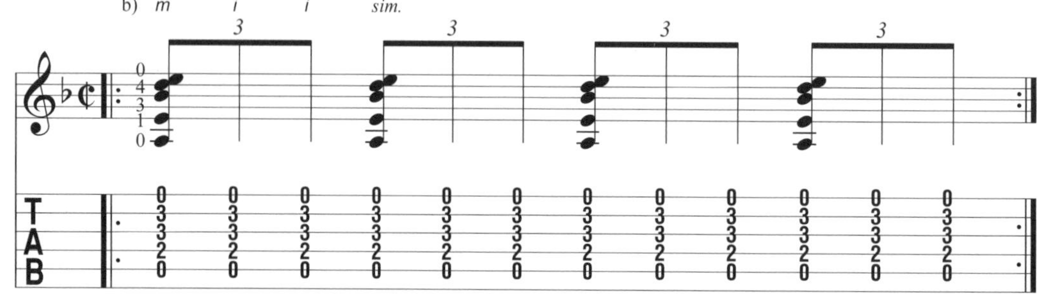

Rajeo Warmup V: Triplets 2

64 55

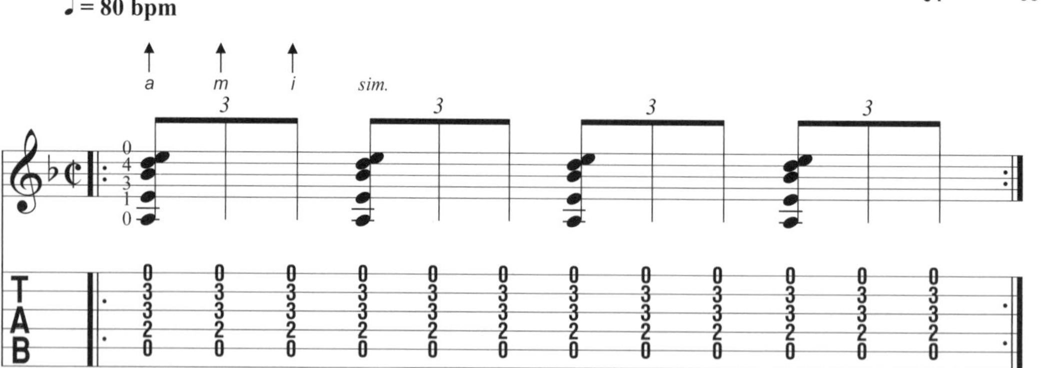

Rajeo Warmup VI: Sixteenth Notes

65 56

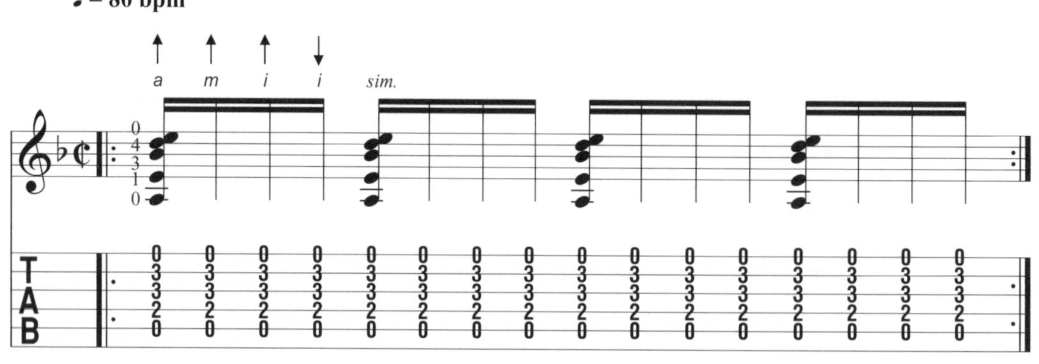

Rajeo Warmup VII: Sixteenth Notes (*e a m i*)

66

57

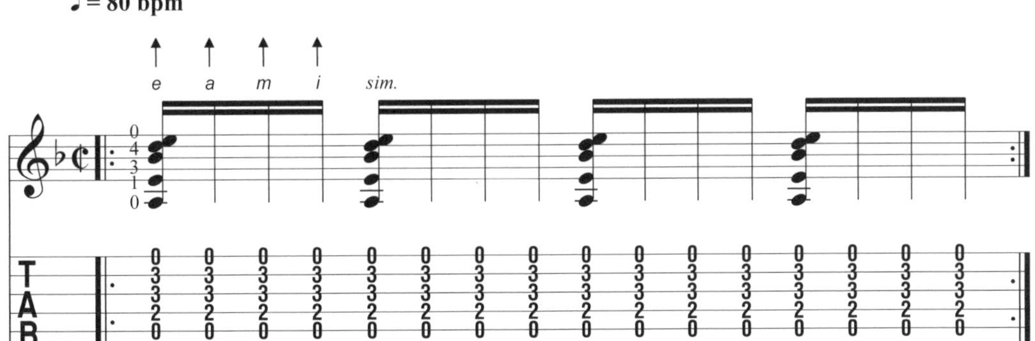

Rajeo Warmup VIII: Quintuplets (*e a m i i*)

67

58

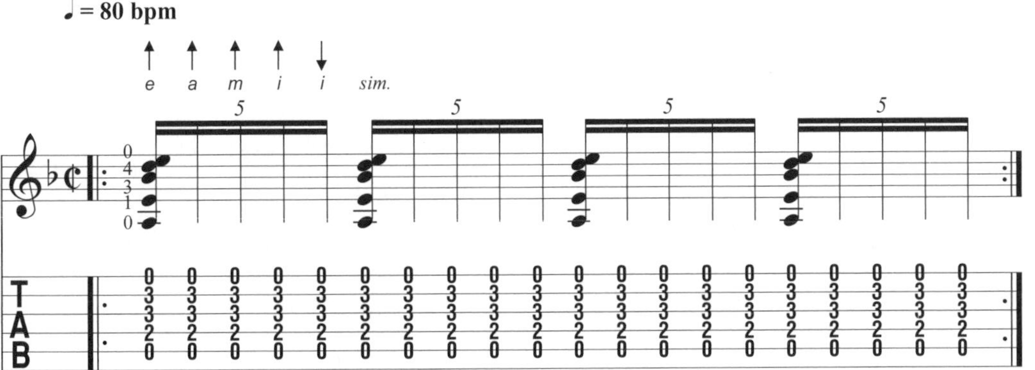

Rajeo Warmup IX: Quintuplets 2 (*p a m i i*)

68

59

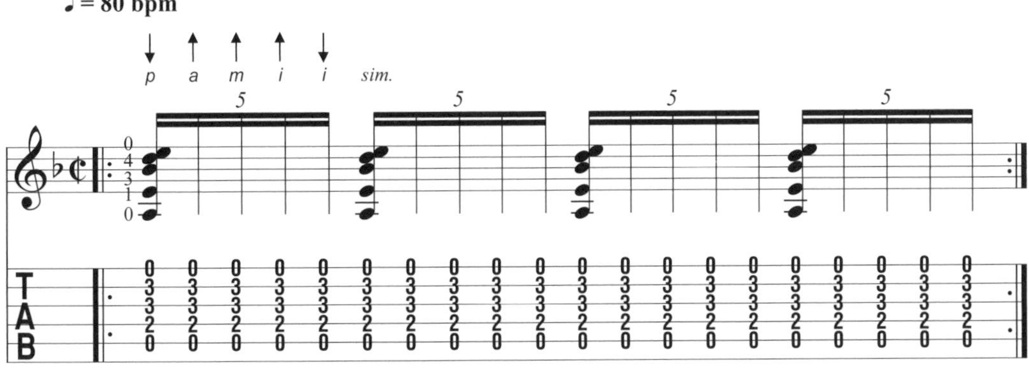

Etudes for rajeo are included in lesson 13, after we discuss *rajeo de abanico*, which is another type of rajeo.

CHAPTER 13

Rajeo de Abanico

FIG. 13.1. Rajeo de Abanico Hand Position

Rajeo de abanico, which translates to "fan," is a type of triplet beat pattern rajeo. The pattern is upstroke, downstroke, downstroke. The first upstroke is played with the thumb's nail, and the remaining two strokes are played with the following fingerings and articulations:

1. *p m p* (thumb nail up, middle nail down, thumb finger down)
2. *p a i* (thumb nail up, ring nail down, index nail down)
3. *p e i* (thumb nail up, pinky nail down, index nail down)

Study these three fingerings, and find the one that you like most and that feels more comfortable. Practice rajeo de abanico with a metronome. Once you master it, you can use it in any of the palos or musical forms.

RAJEO DE ABANICO WARMUP EXERCISES

Rajeo de Abanico Warmup I

69 60

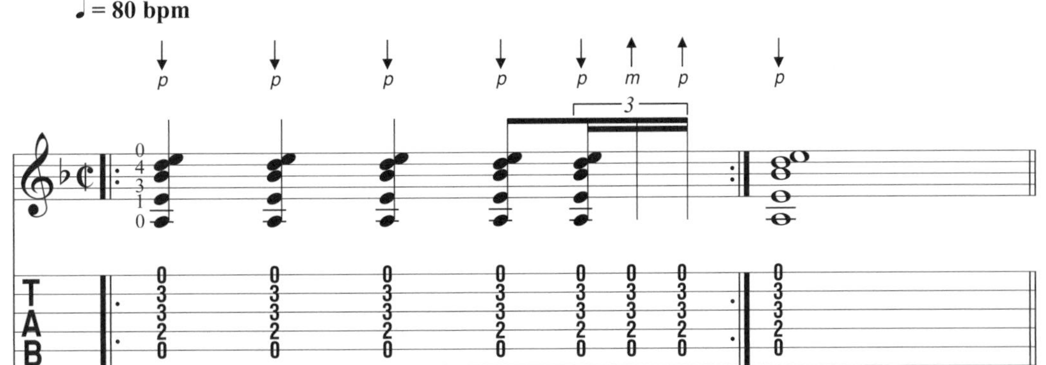

Rajeo de Abanico Warmup II

70 61

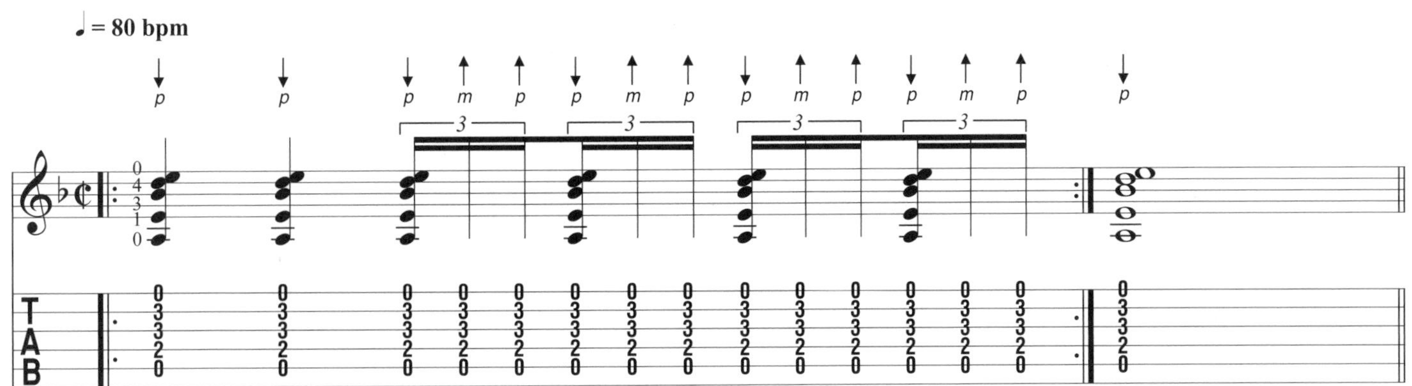

Rajeo de Abanico Warmup III

71 62

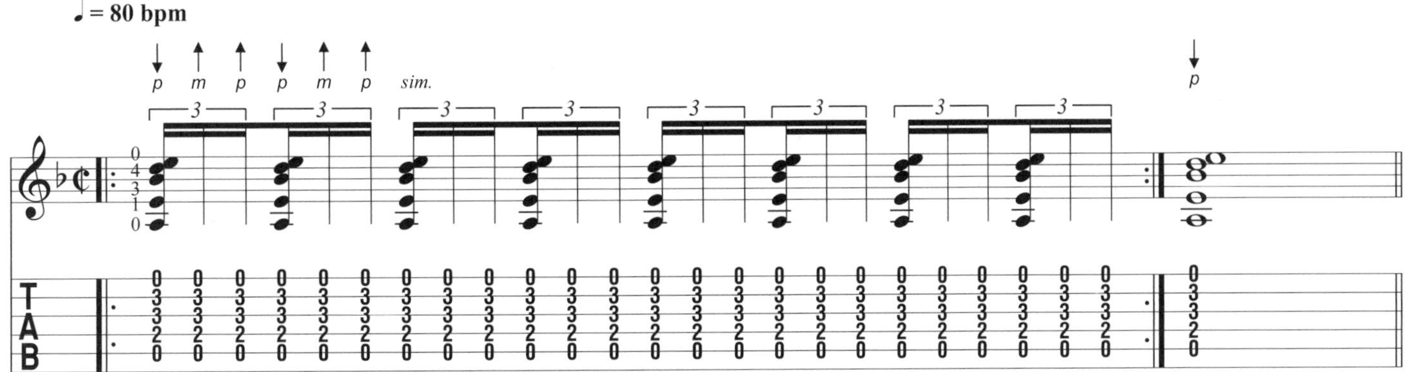

RAJEO PALO ETUDES

Tangos

72 63

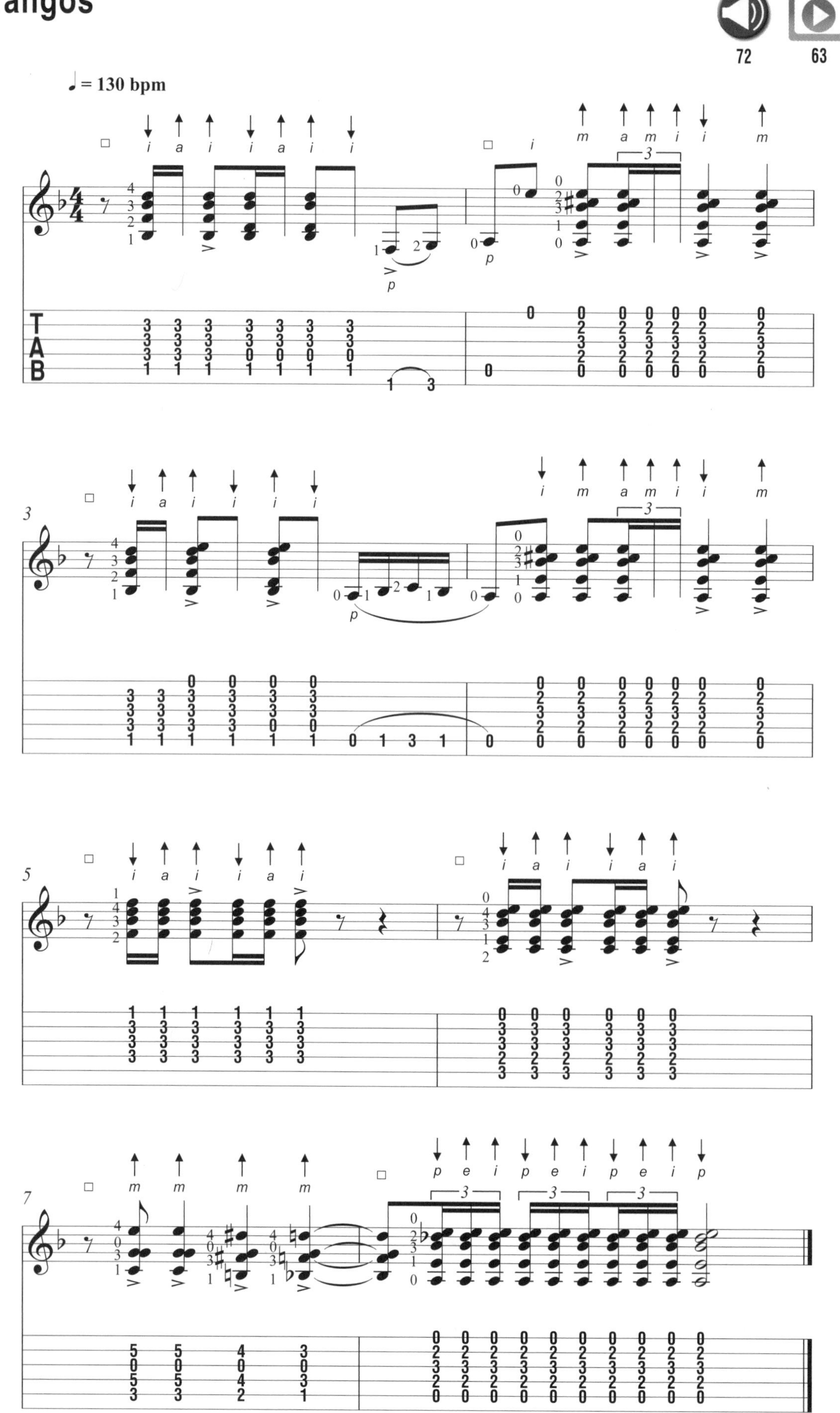

Soleá

73 64

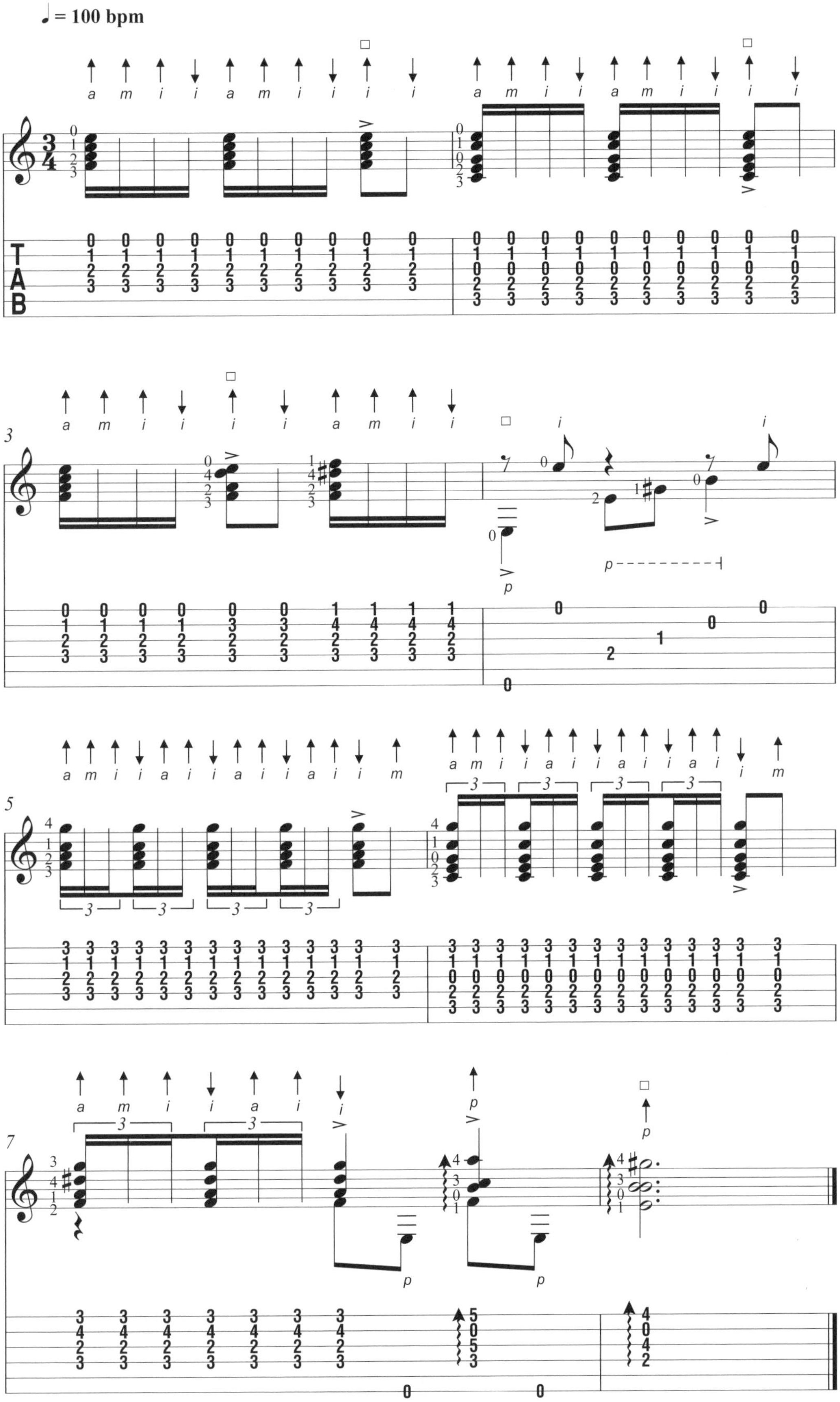

♩ = 100 bpm

Soleá por Bulerías

74 65

♩ = 125 bpm

CHAPTER 14

Trémolo

FIG. 14.1. Trémolo Hand Position

The flamenco *trémolo* is a rapid succession of five notes, performed as follows:

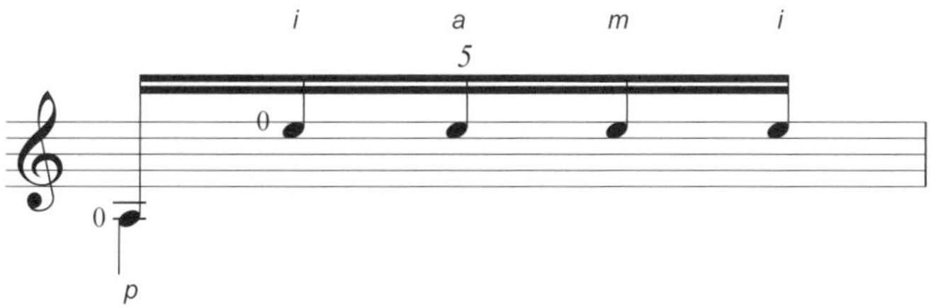

FIG. 14.2. Five-Note Trémolo

The traditional flamenco trémolo is played as a quintuplet. The sequence is *p-i-a-m-i*, and the thumb is again placed on the adjacent string (*apoyando*) after sounding its note. It has one note more than the tremolo used in classical guitar technique, which uses one bass note per three upper notes. In flamenco trémolo, for each bass note, we play four notes in the upper voice, which can be performed on the first, second, or third strings. Finger movements come from the knuckles of the hand and not from the middle knuckles of the fingers.

The use of a metronome will help you to master this flamenco guitar technique. Focus on playing each individual note clearly and at the same volume.

TRÉMOLO WARMUP EXERCISES

Trémolo Warmup I

75

66

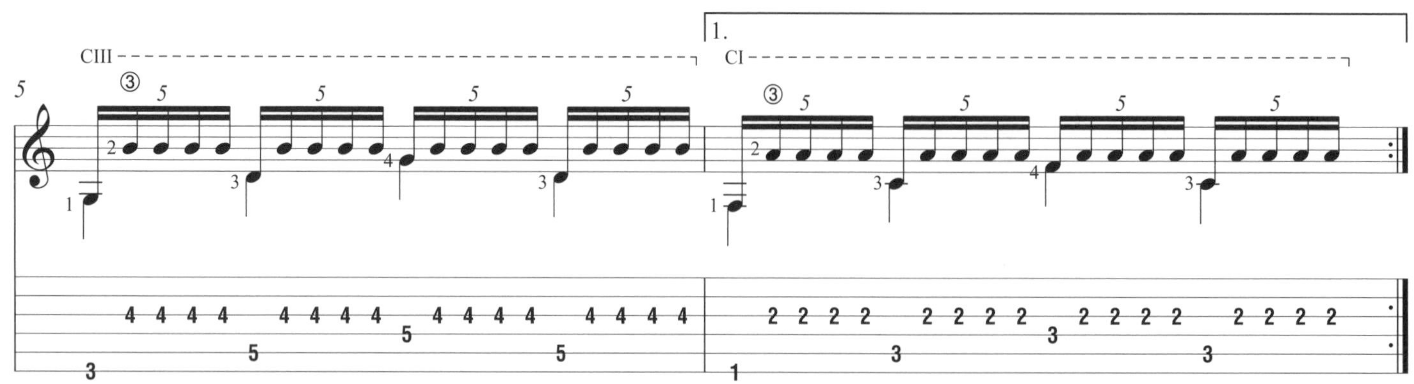

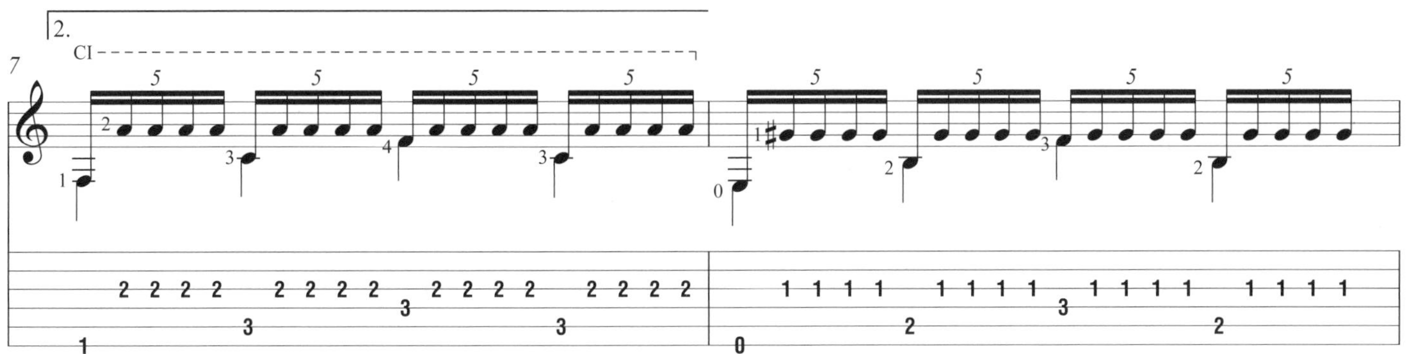
2.
CI

Trémolo Warmup II

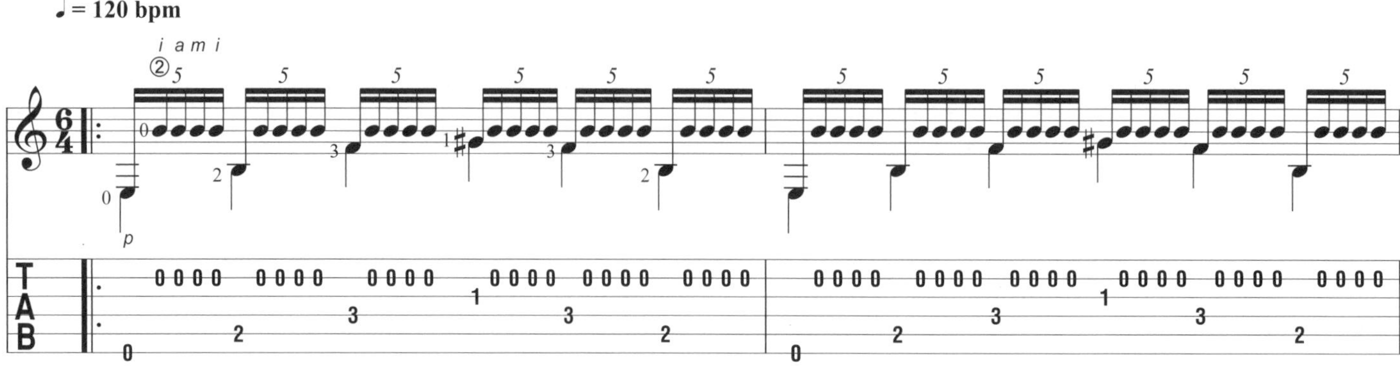

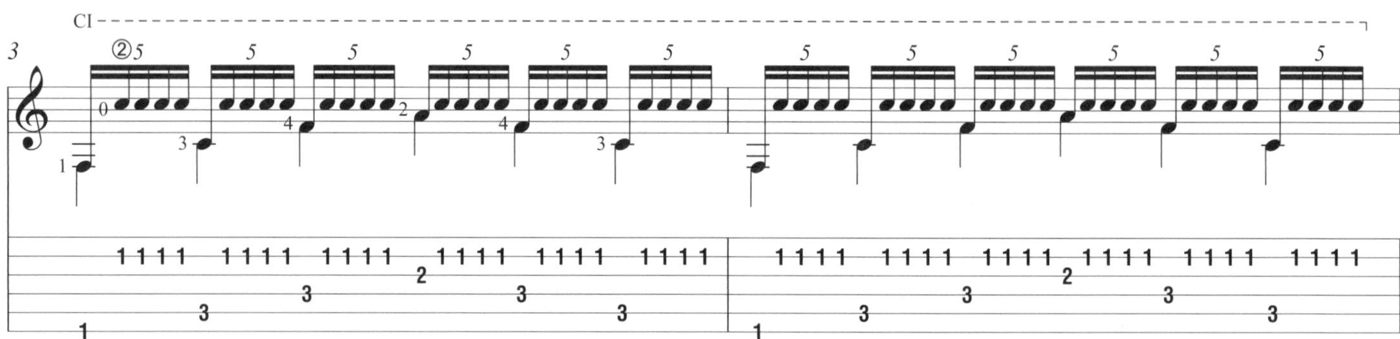

2.
CI

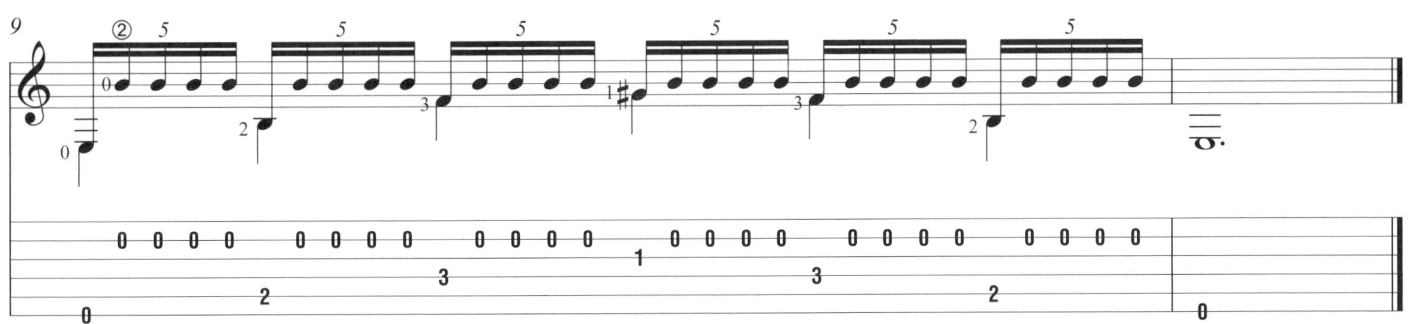

Trémolo Warmup III

2.
CI
7

8

9

TRÉMOLO PALO ETUDE

Soleá

Moderato

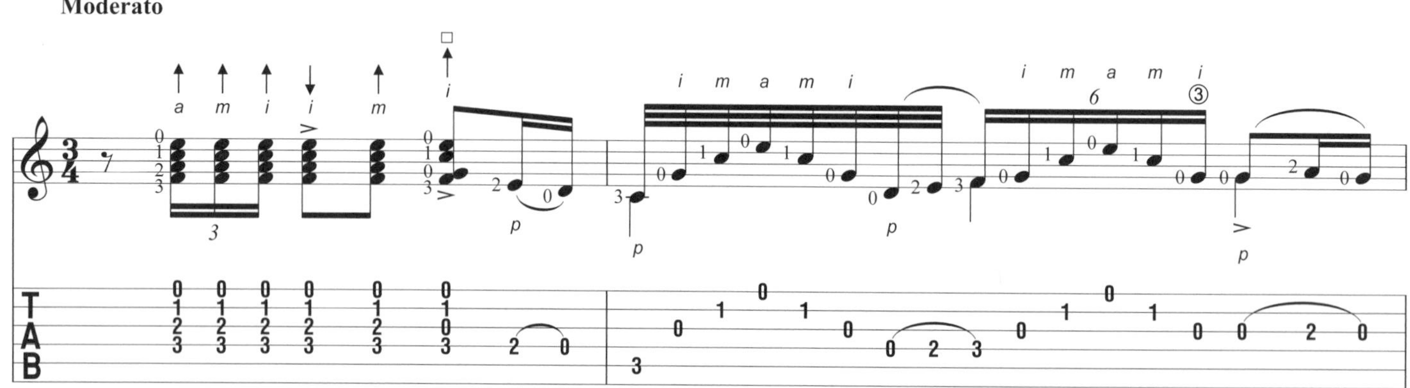

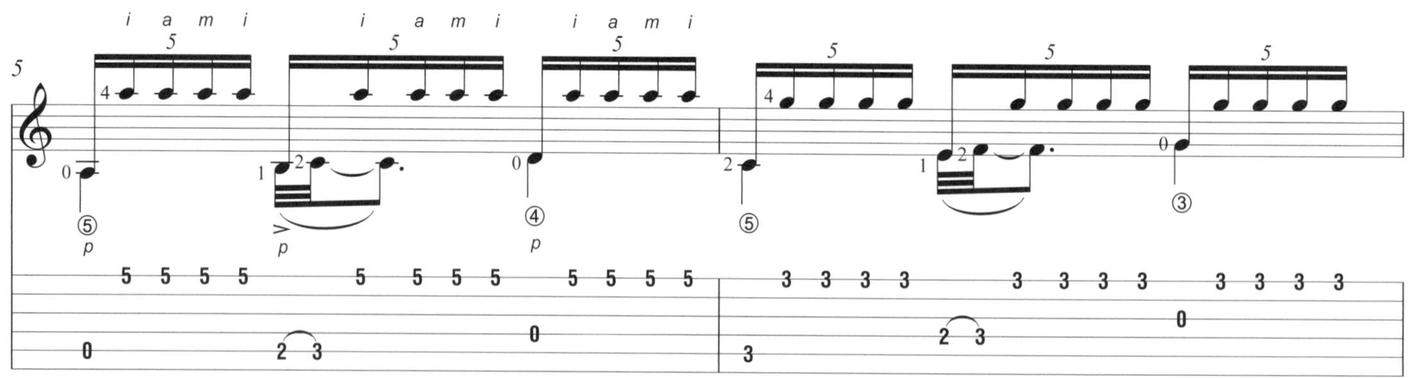

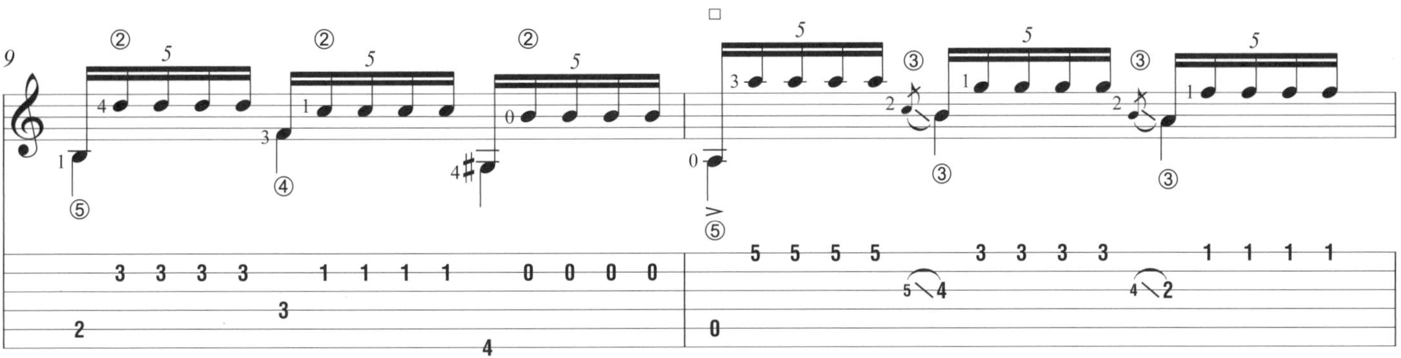

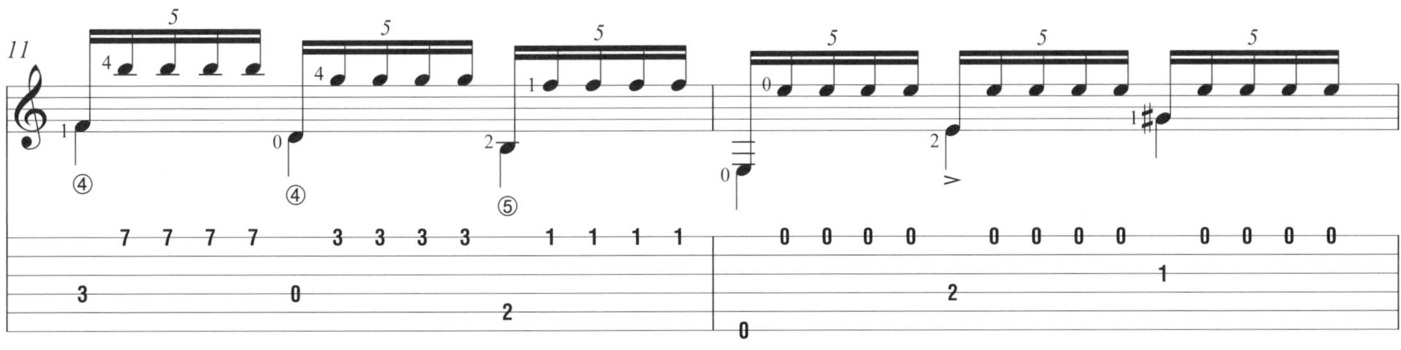

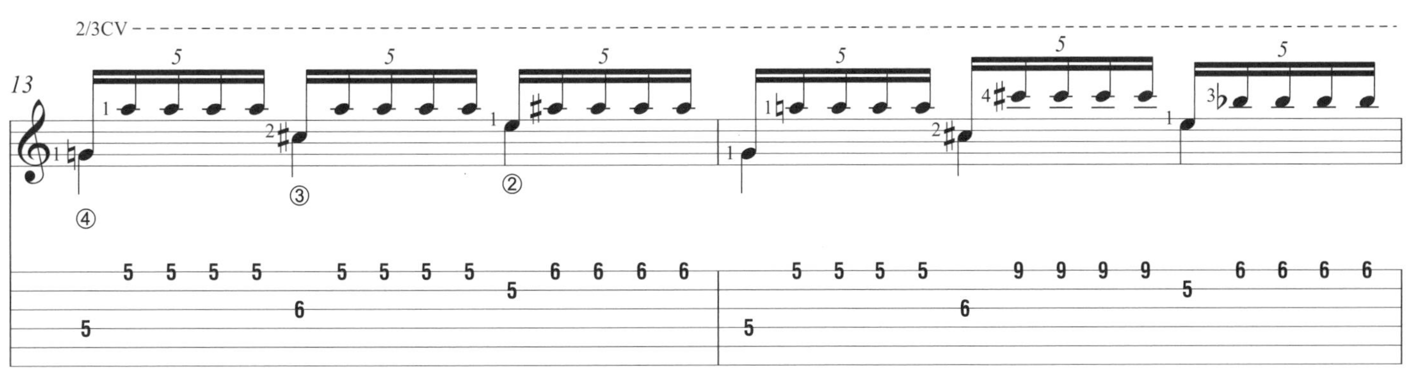
2/3CV

Rubato
2/3CV
A tempo
5/6CV

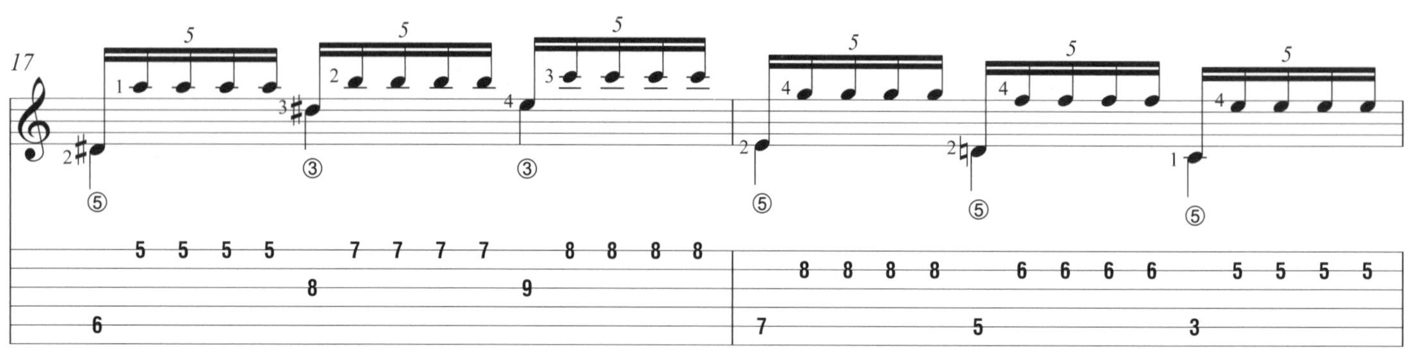

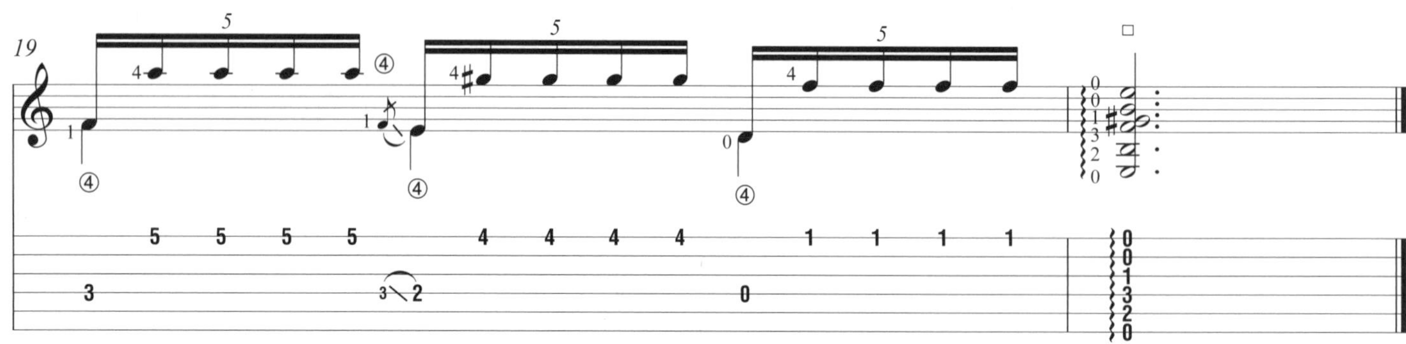

PART III

Falsetas

The following falsetas are etudes that incorporate the techniques presented in part II of this book. Media tracks for each falseta include full performances (both audio and video) and percussion-only play-along audio tracks that you can use to practice the guitar part. The first page of this book includes a special code that will you grant you access to the media files at www.halleonard.com/mylibrary. This site includes a playback tool that will allow you to adjust the tempo of any audio track to suit your preference. Practice slowly at first, and then bring the your performance up to the indicated tempo.

SOLEÁ

Soleá I

Featured Techniques: arpegio, pulgar, golpe, and pulgar/índice.

Capo I

♩ = 100 bpm

Soleá II

Featured Techniques: arpegio, pulgar, and alzapúa.

♩ = 100 bpm

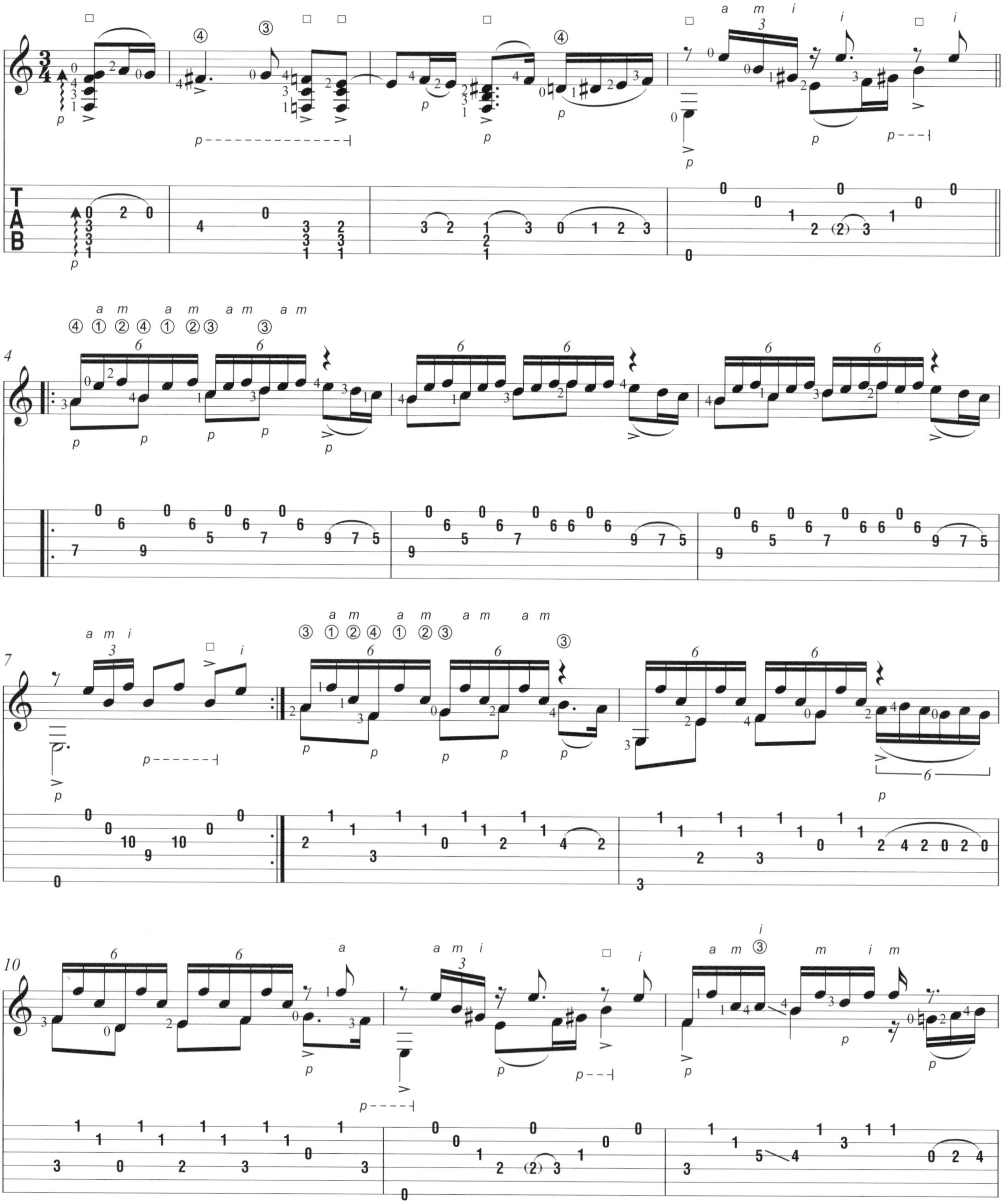

Soleá III

Featured Techniques: arpegio, ligado, and alzapúa.

83, 84

72

Capo I

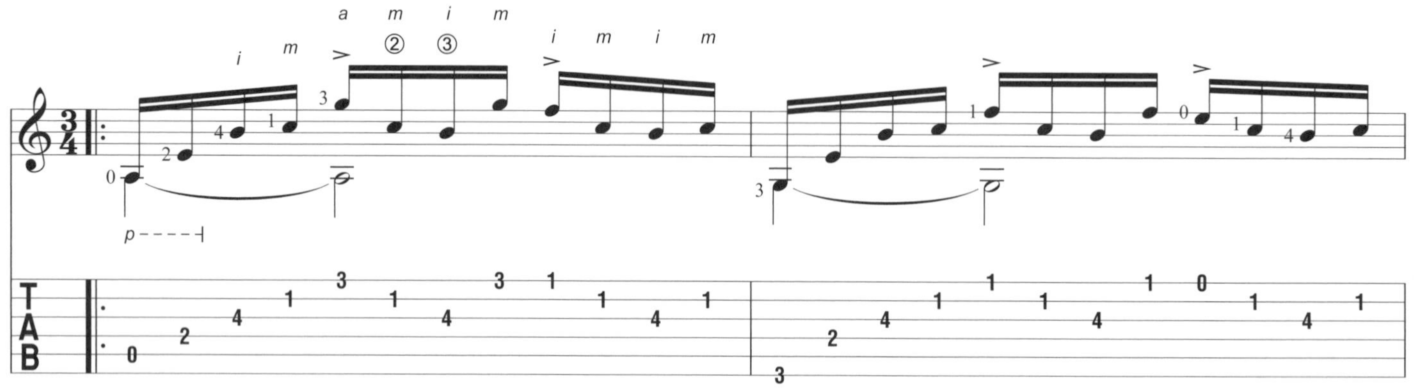

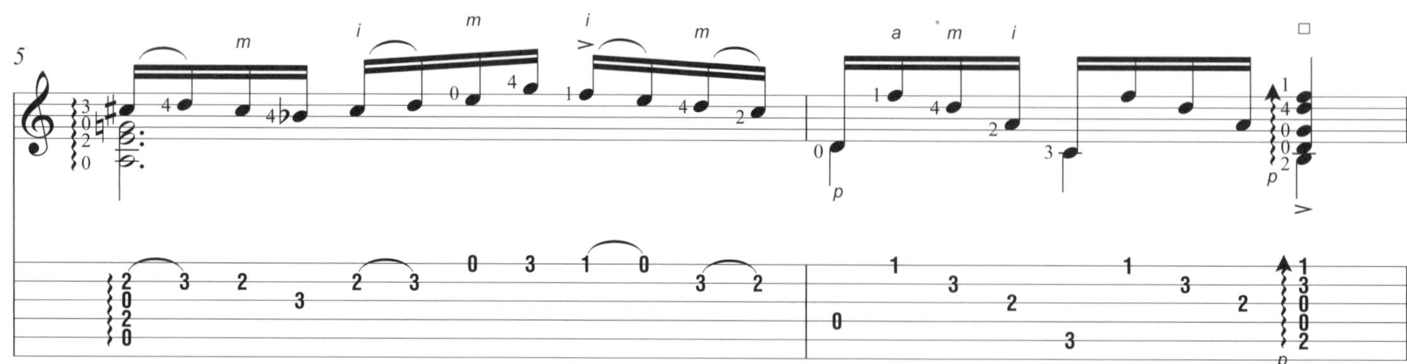

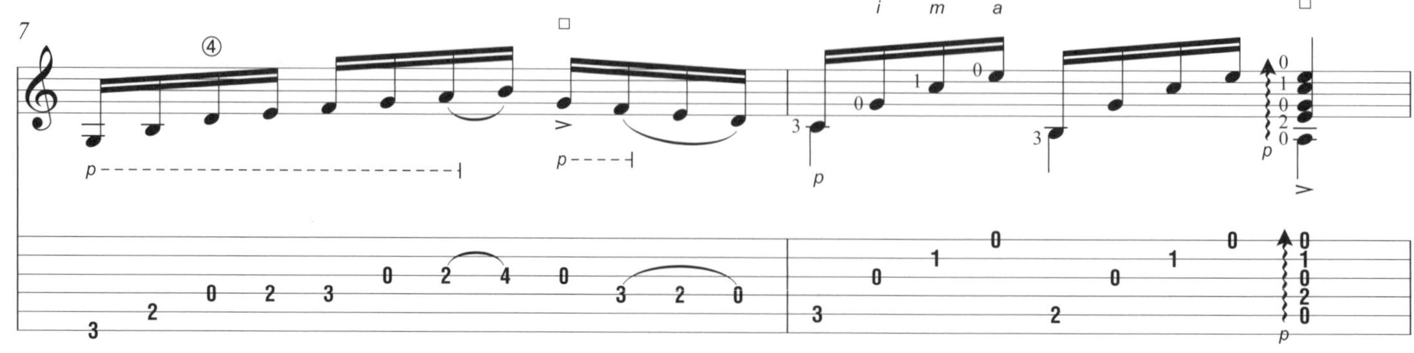

Soleá IV

Featured Techniques: rajeo, ligado, and pulgar.

85, 86

73

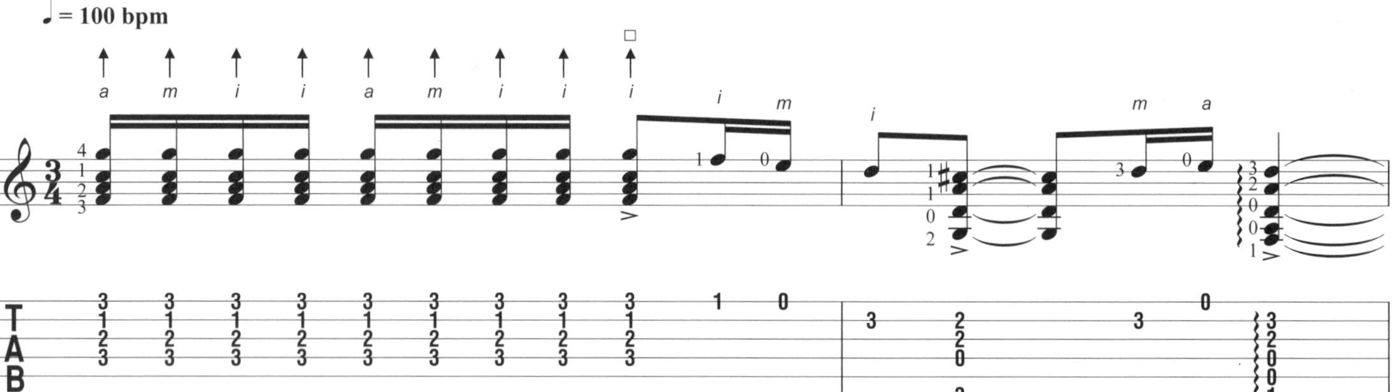

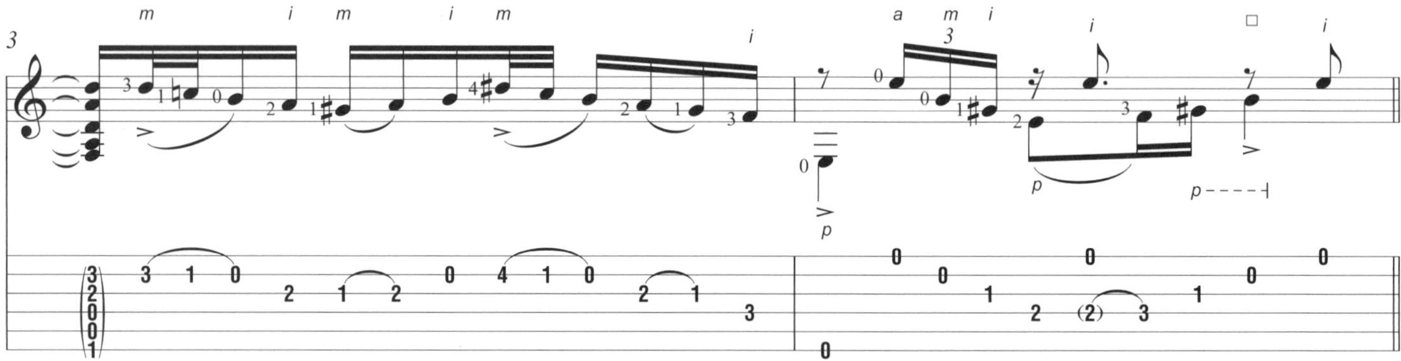

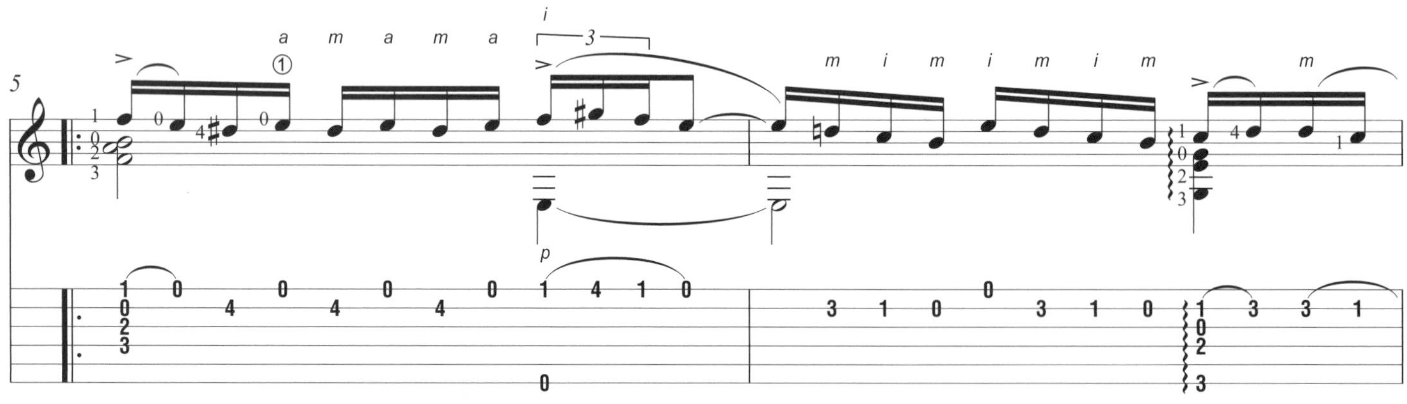

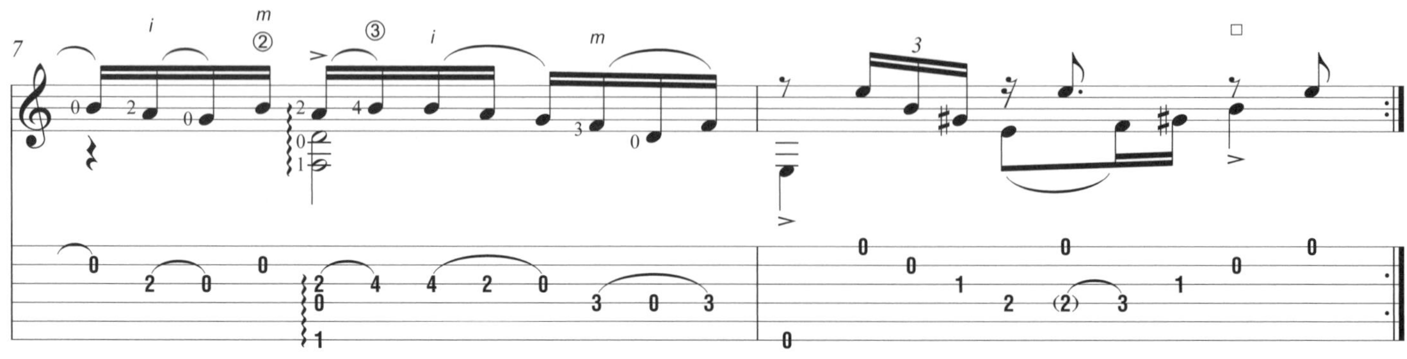

9
11
CV
13
15
5/6CVIII

Toda una Vida, directed by Alfonso Queipo de Llano, 2014. Singers: Rancapino and Cañeta de Málaga; Guitar: Antonio Soto; Dancer: Carrete de Malaga. Photo by Diego Gallardo

FANDANGOS DE HUELVA

Fandangos de Huelva I

87, 88 74

Featured Techniques: rajeo, arpegio, and alzapúa

Capo II

♩ = 140 bpm

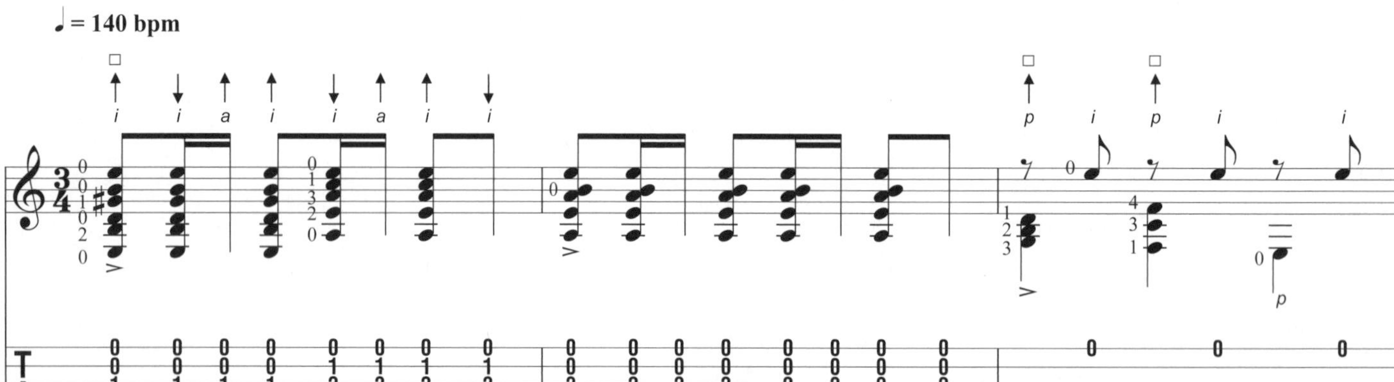

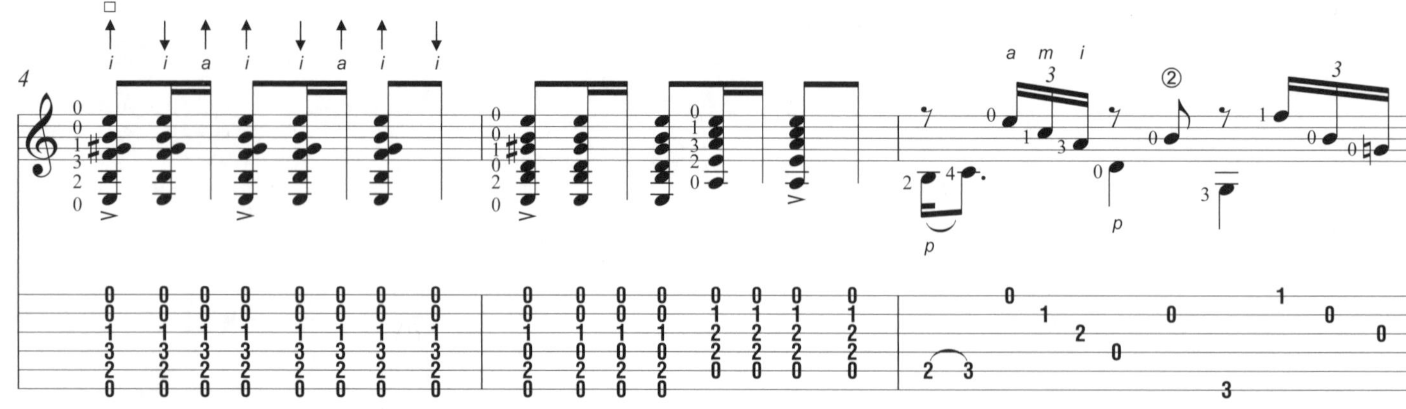

10
13
16
19

Fandangos de Huelva II

Featured Techniques: arpegio and ligado

Capo II

♩ = 140 bpm

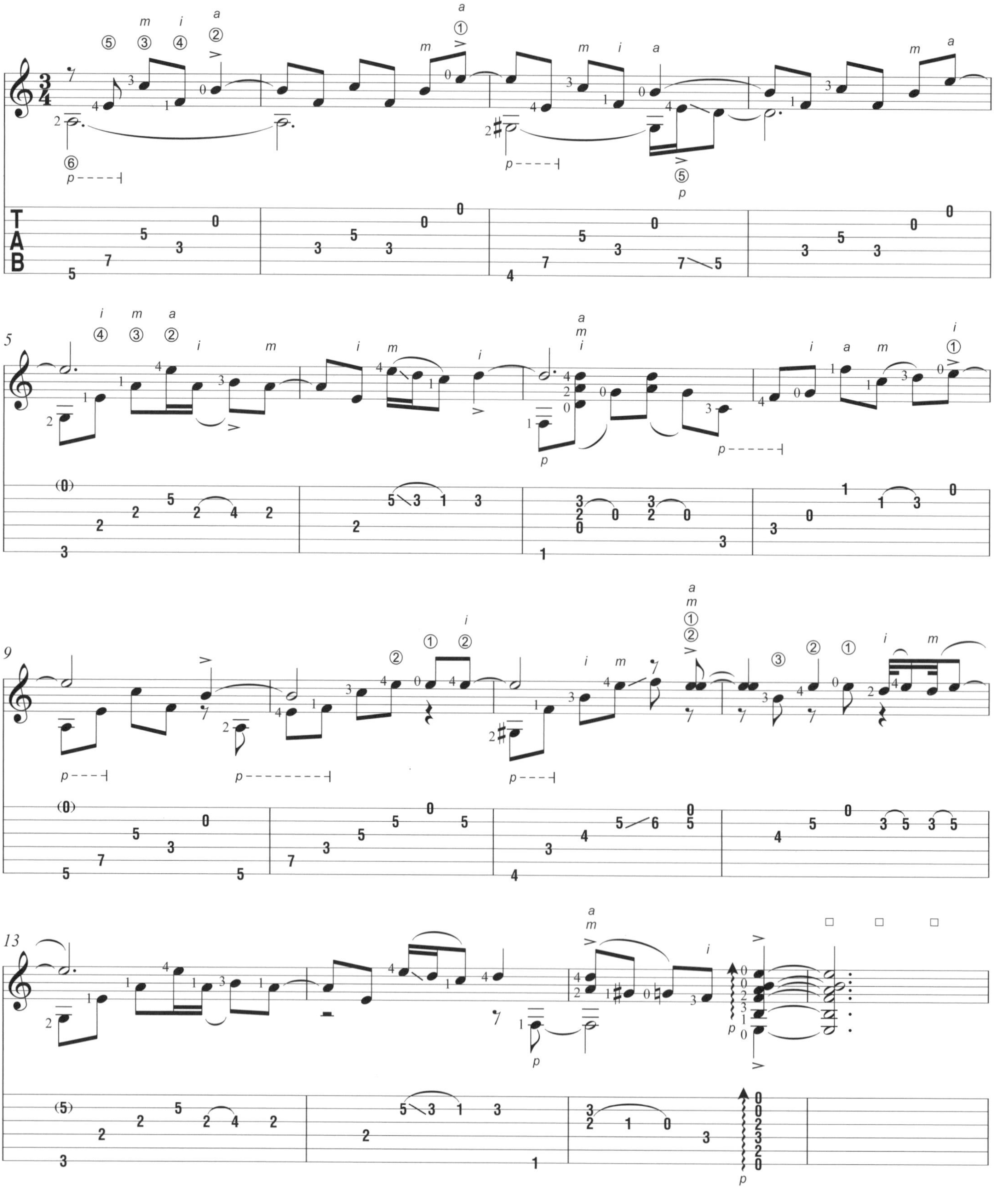

Fandangos de Huelva III

Featured Techniques: picado, arpegio, and ligado

91, 92

76

Capo II

♩ = 140 bpm

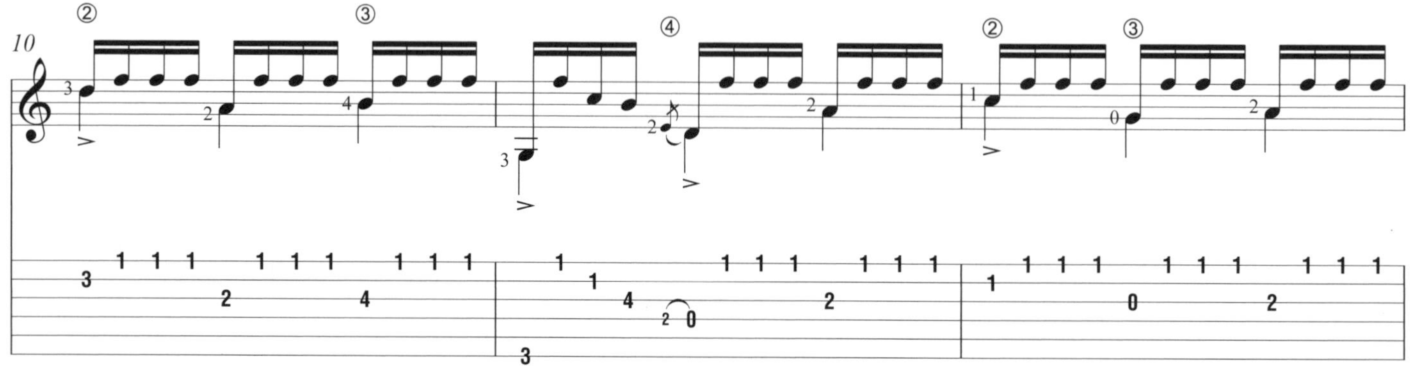

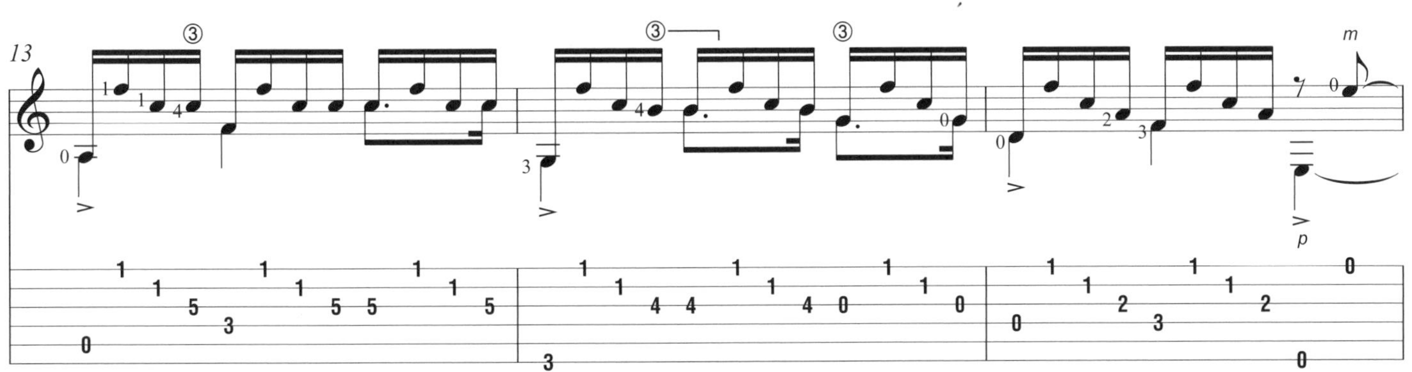
13
③
③
③
m
p

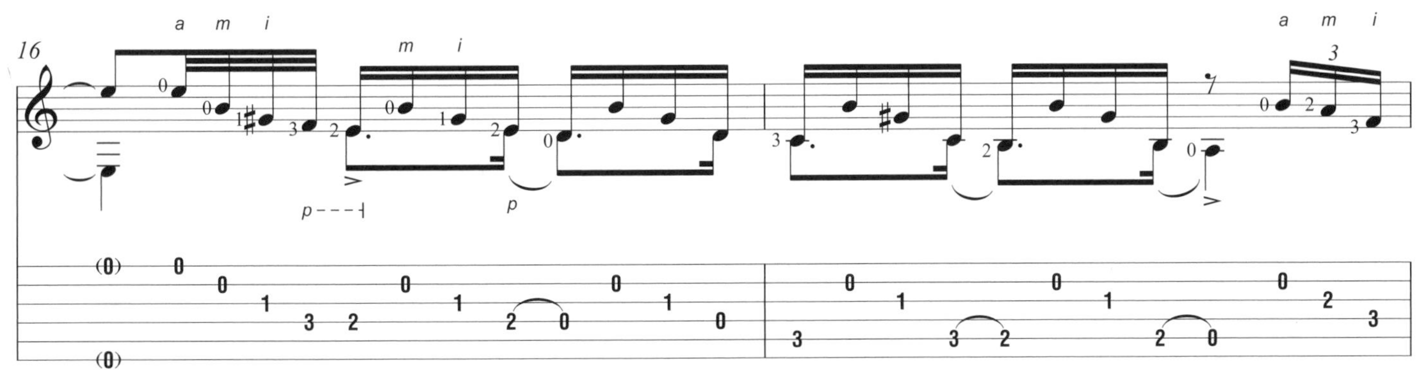
16
a m i
m i
p
p
a m i
3

18
i
p
p

Fandangos de Huelva IV

Featured Techniques: rajeo and alzapúa

93, 94

77

Capo II

♩ = 140 bpm

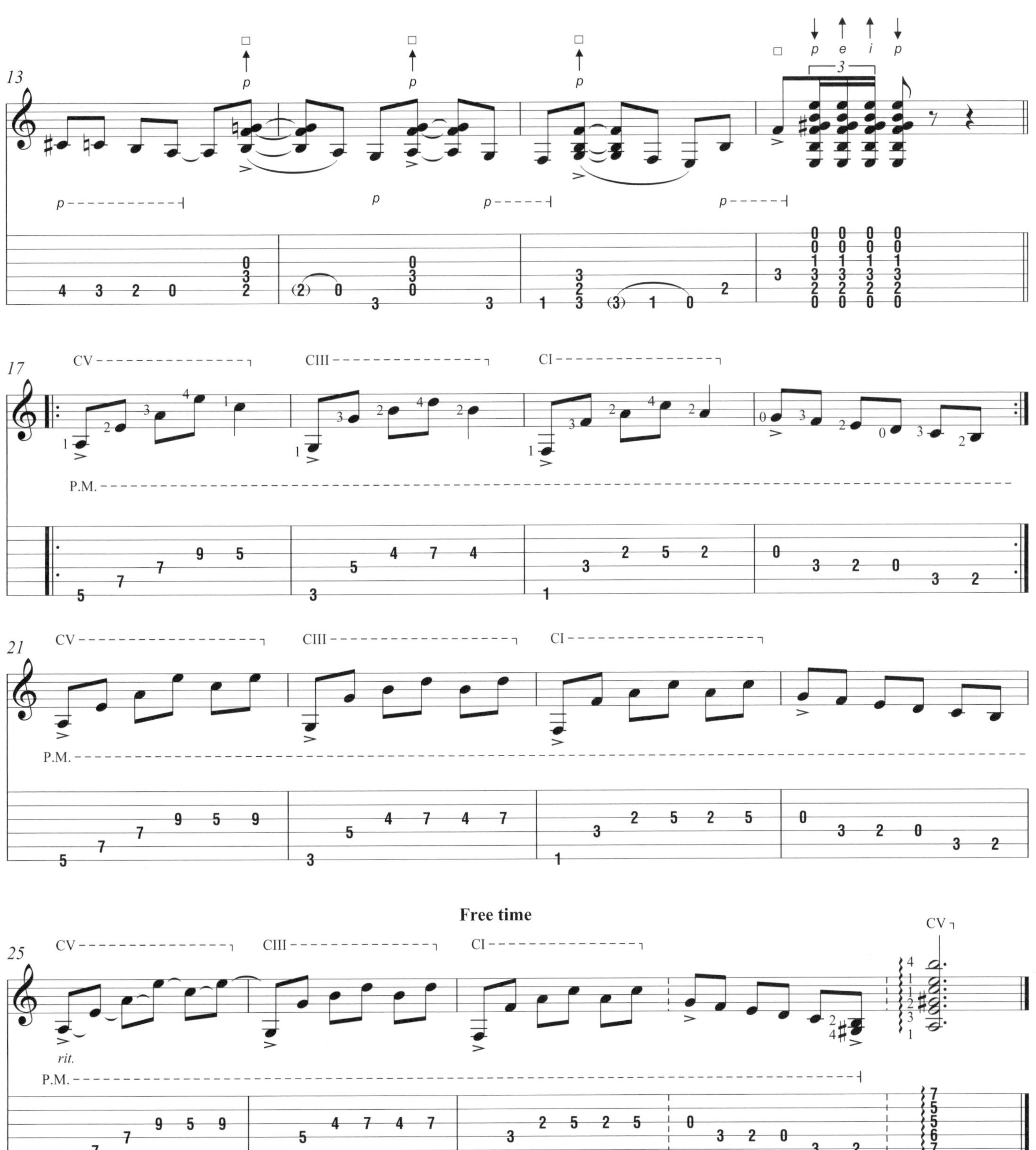
13
17
CV
CIII
CI
P.M.
21
25
Free time
rit.

GUAJIRA

Guajira I

Featured Techniques: picado and ligado

95, 96

78

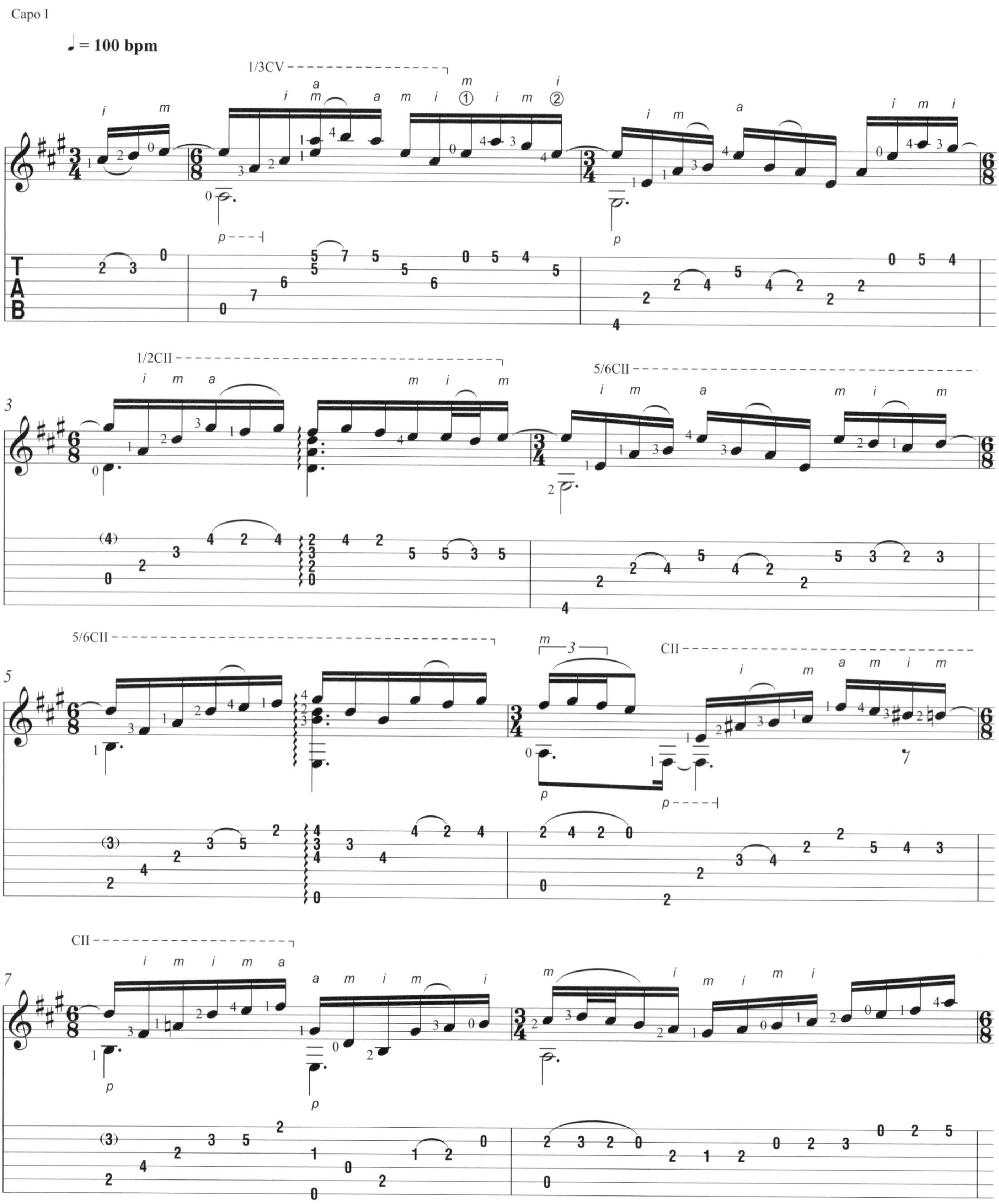

Capo I

♩ = 100 bpm

Guajira II

Featured Techniques: arpegio and ligado

♩ = 100 bpm

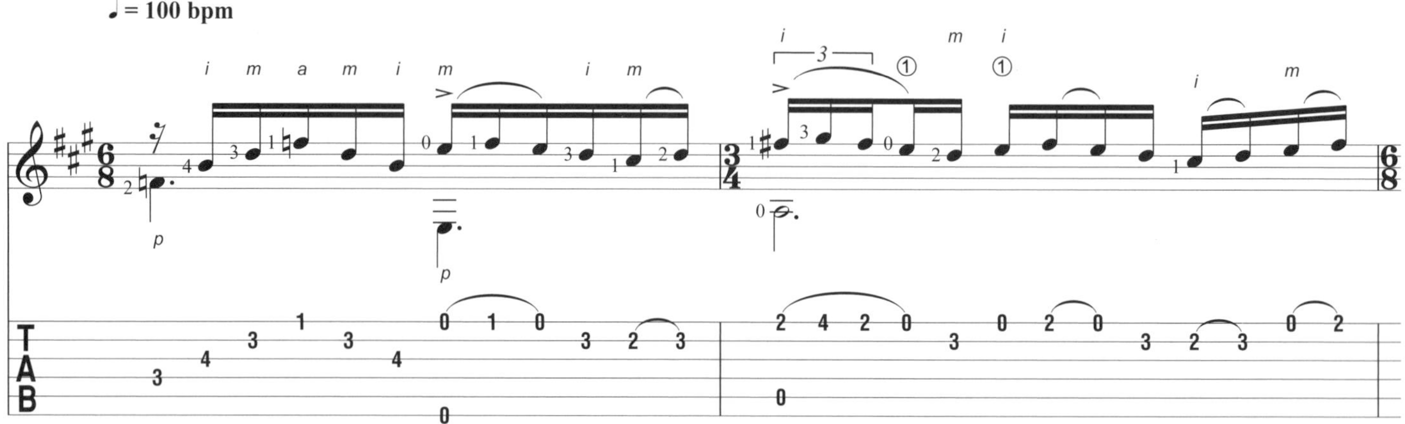

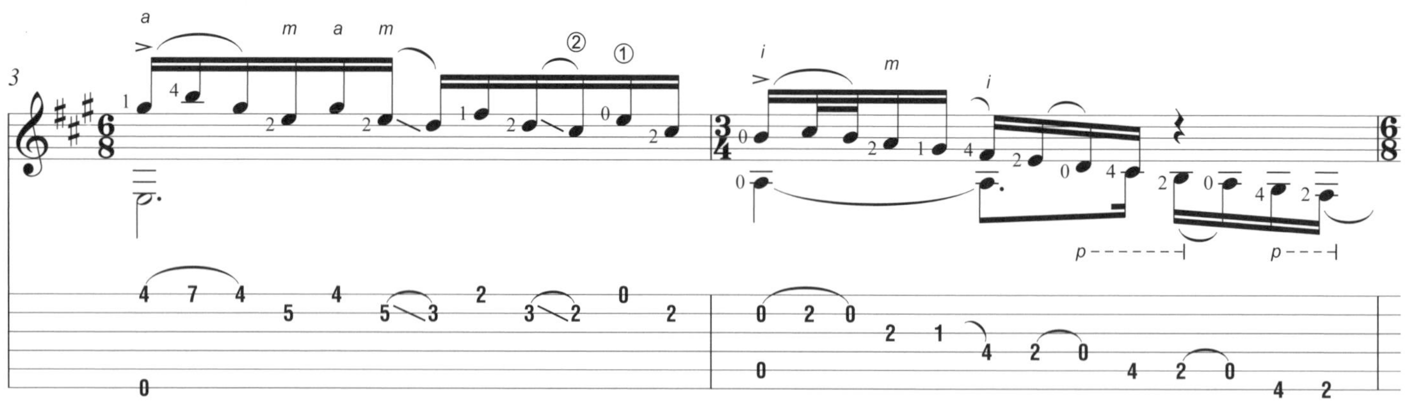

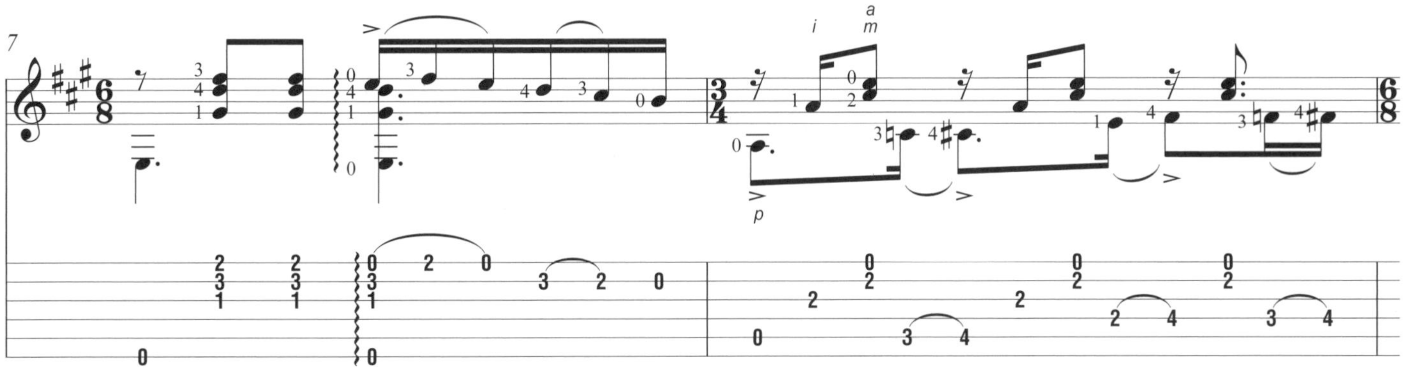
7
i
a
m
p

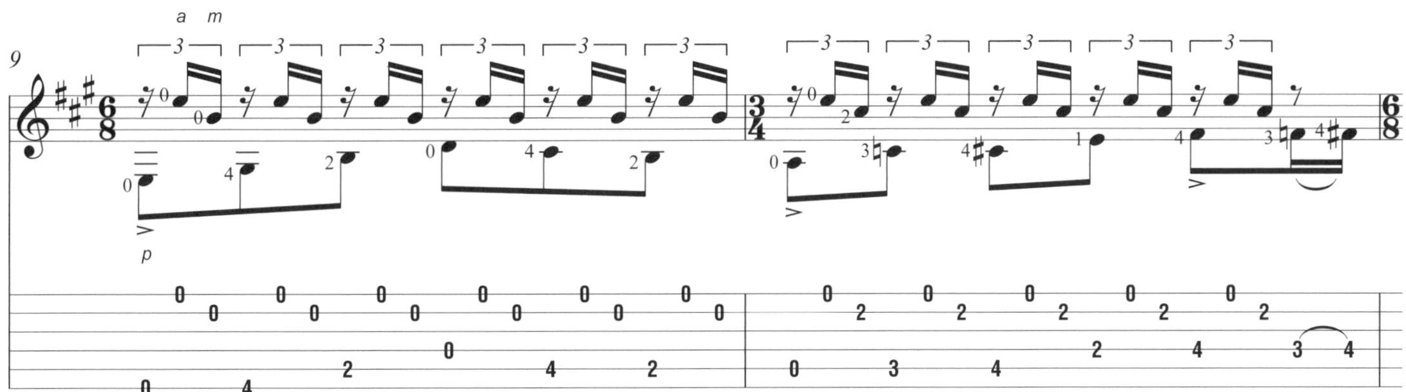
9
a m
p

2/3CII
11
p

Guajira III

Featured Techniques: picado, ligado, and arpegio

Capo I

♩ = 100 bpm

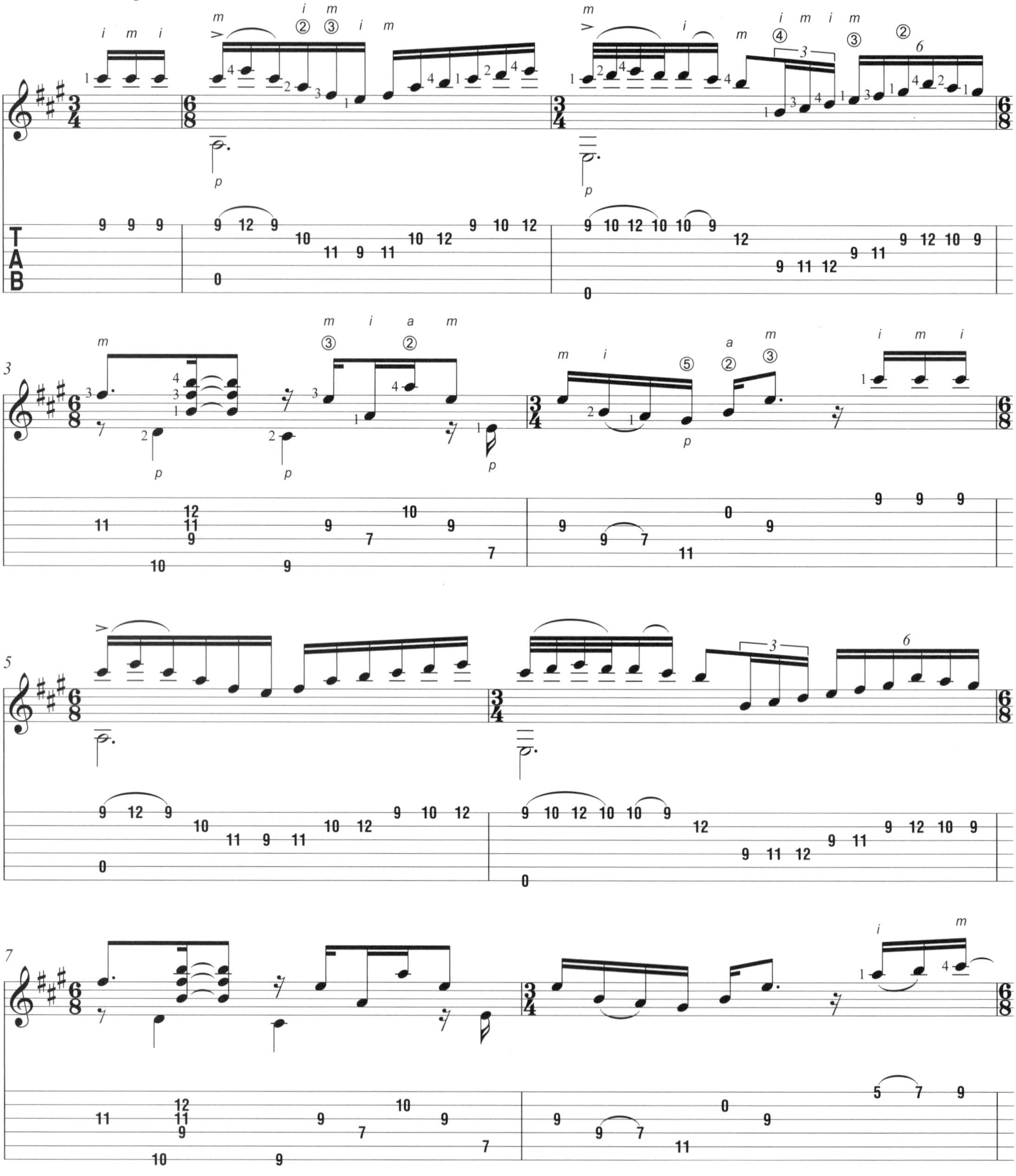

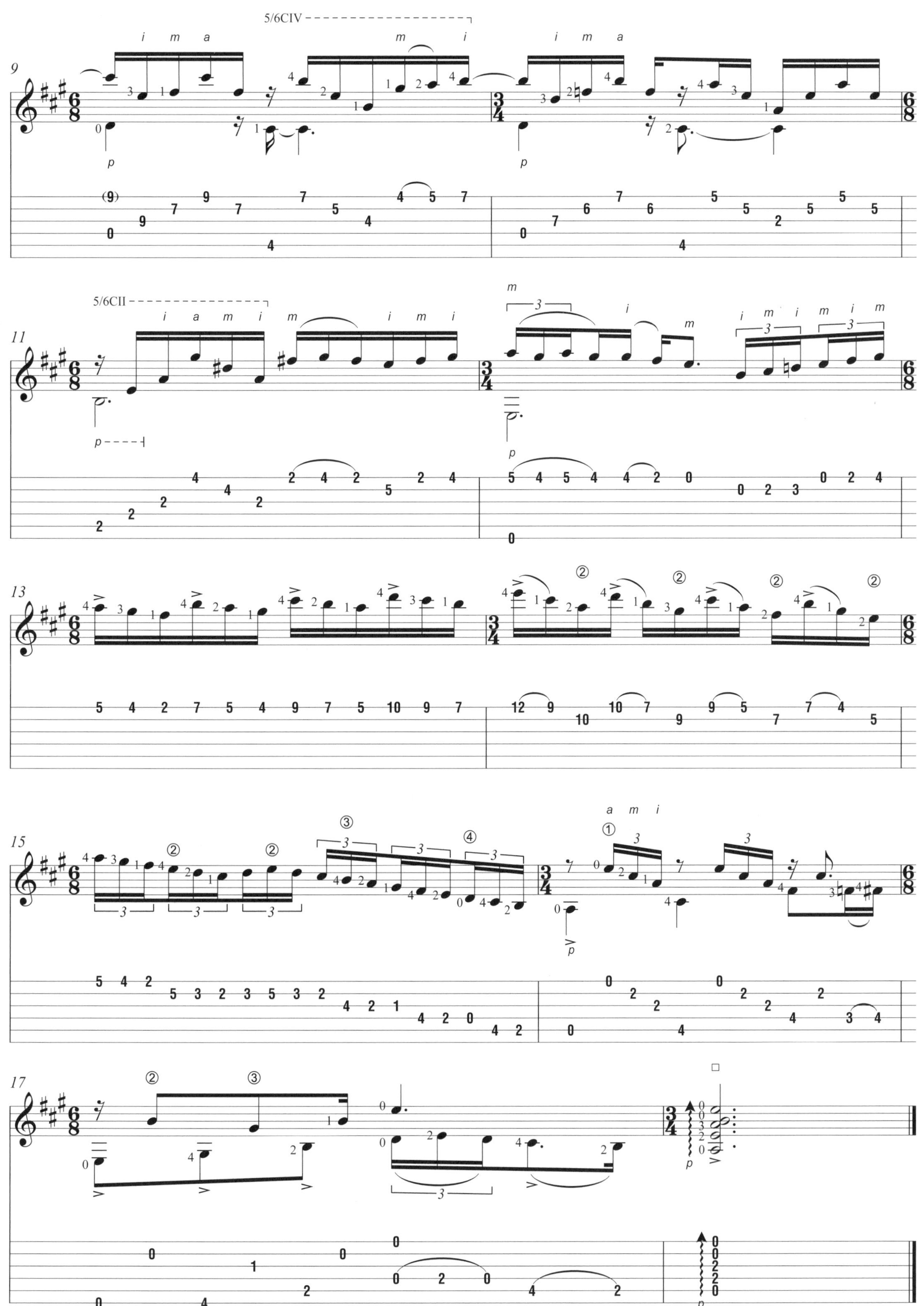
5/6CIV
5/6CII

Guajira IV

Featured Technique: arpegio

101, 102

81

Capo I

♩ = 100 bpm

BULERÍAS

Bulerías I

Featured Techniques: rajeo, pulgar, pulgar/índice, arpegio, and golpe

Capo III

♩ = 110 bpm

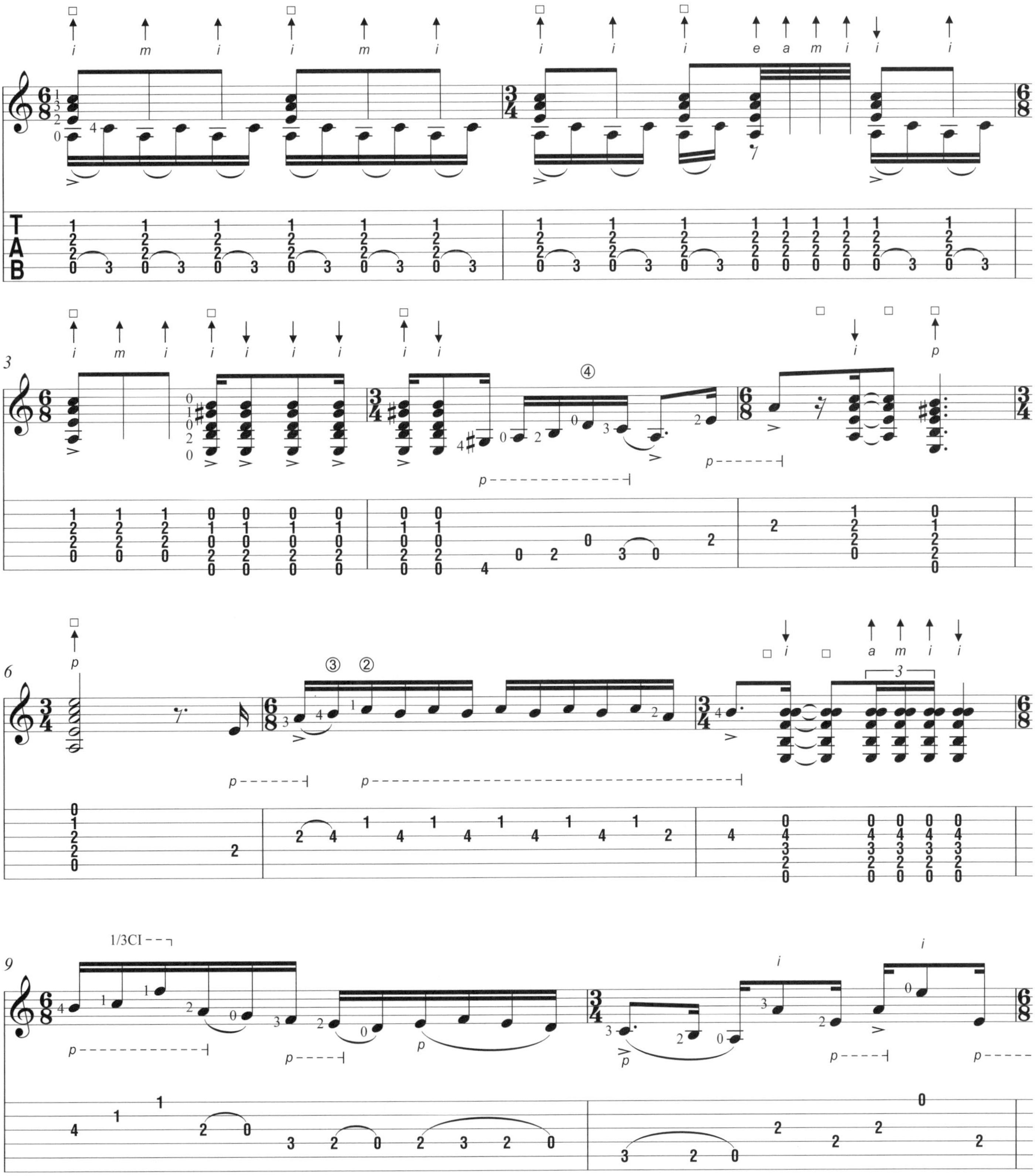

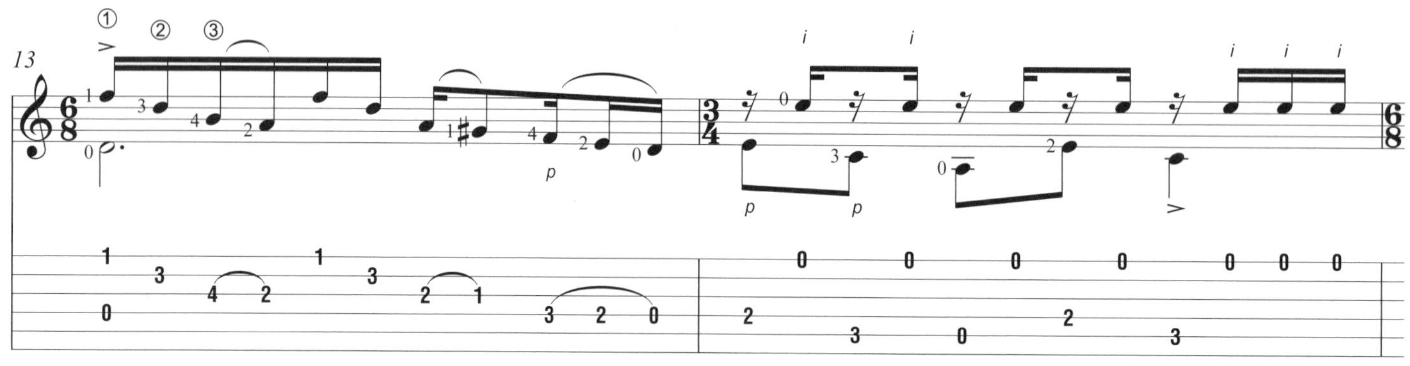

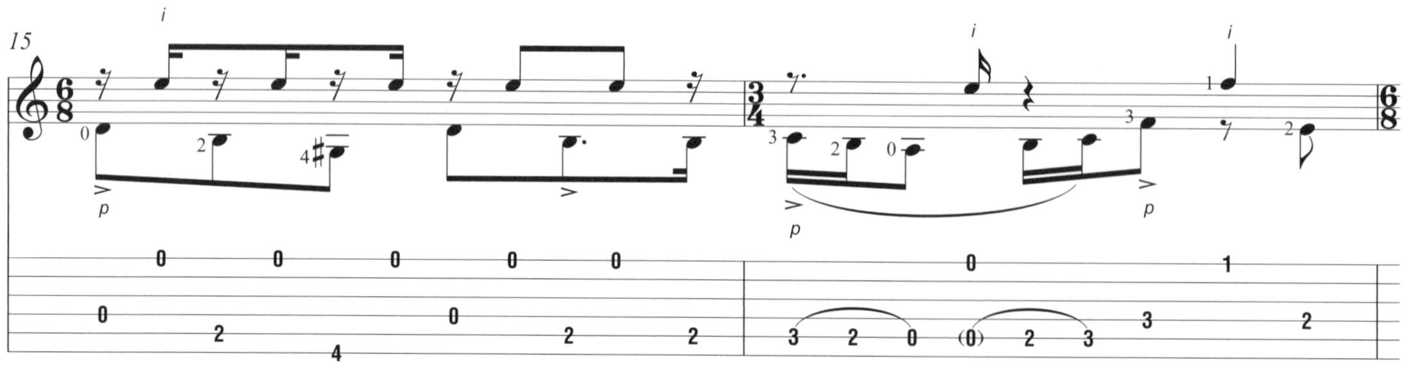

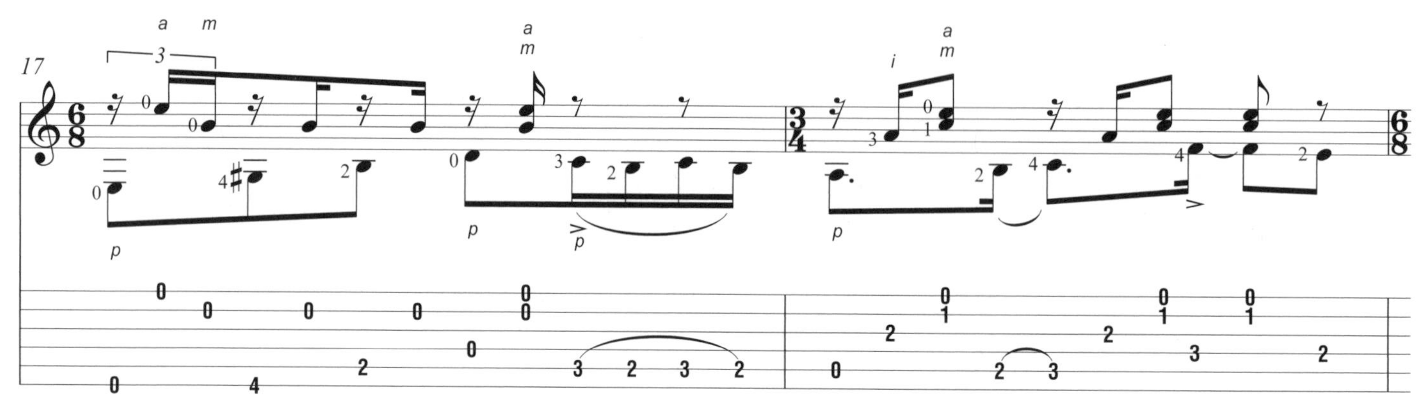

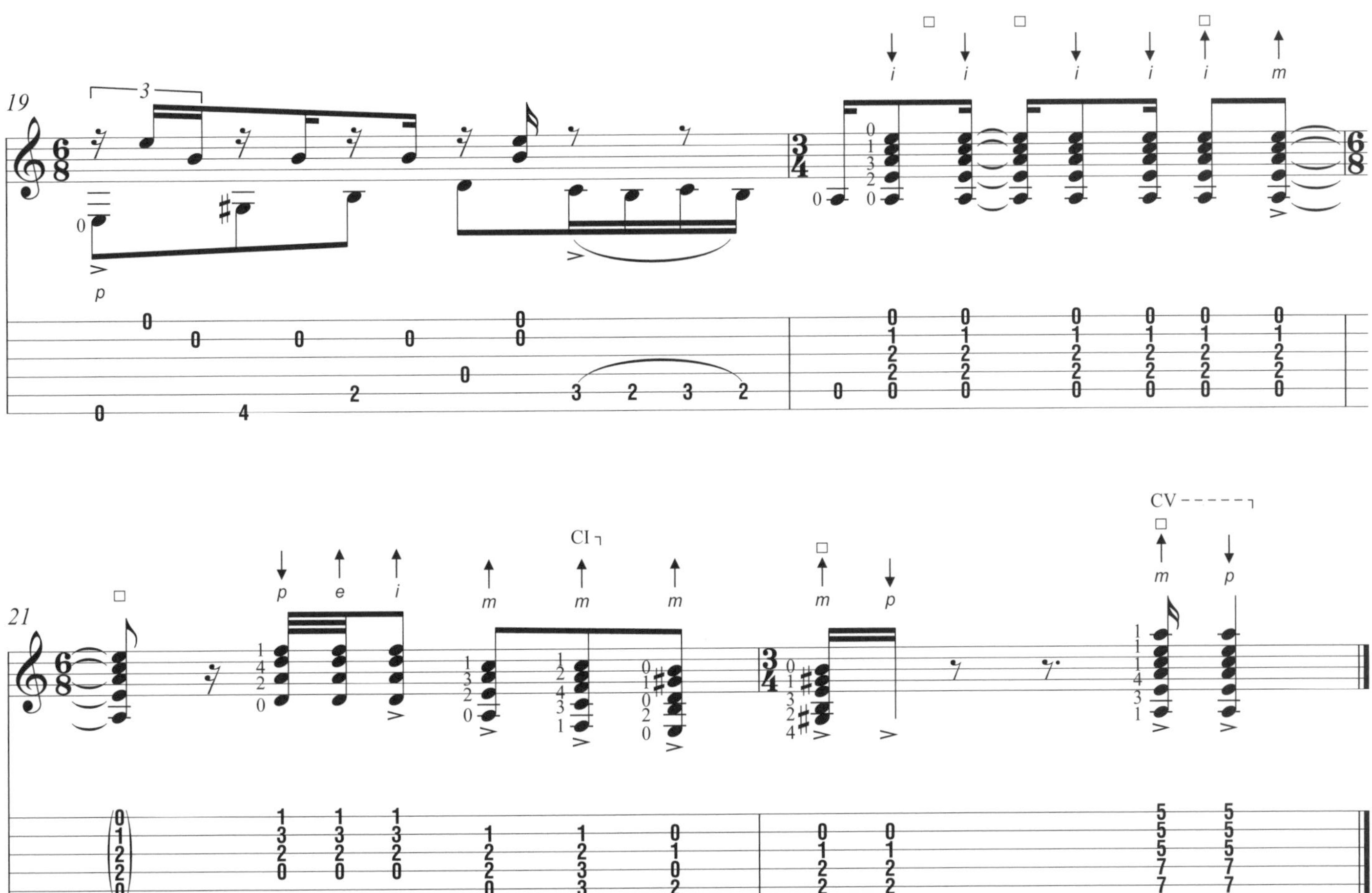

"Esencia de Rojas y Rodríguez" by Ángel Rojas and Carlos Rodríguez, 2017. Percussion: Agapula; Singer: Rocío Bazán and Chelo Pantoja; Guitar: Luis Miguel Manzano; Dancer: Miguel Ángel Rojas. Photo by Beatrix Mexi Molnar.

Bulerías II

Featured Techniques: ligado, golpe, pulgar, and pulgar/índice

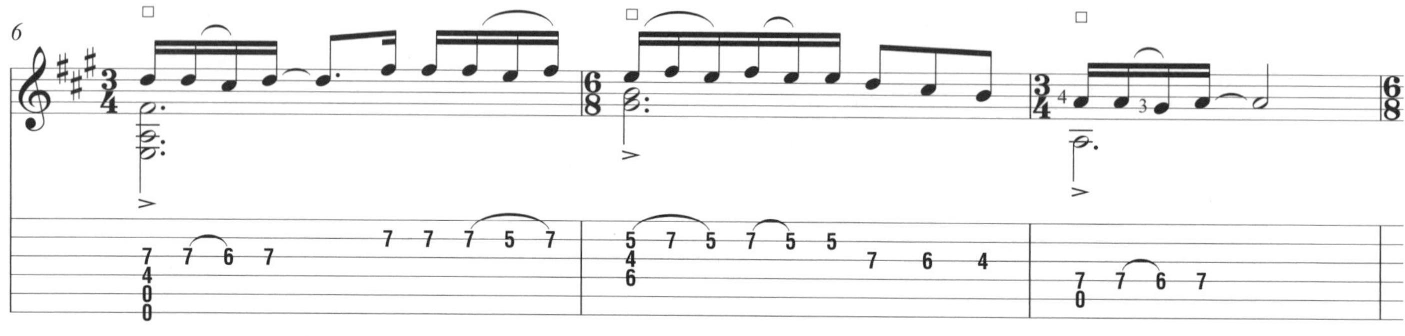

CI
CV

Bulerías III

Featured Techniques: rajeo, arpegio, pulgar, ligado, and golpe

107, 108

84

Capo III

♩ = 110 bpm

2/3CII
p
p
p
2/3CII
i
i
i
i
i
p

“Impulso” by José Porcel, 2020. Dancers: Marta Gálvez and Isabel Rodríguez; Singer: David Vázquez and Pedro Obregón; Guitar: Álvaro Martinete and Víctor Márquez; Percussion: Javier Fernández; Violin: Fernando Rico. Photo by Beatrix Mexi Molnar.

ALEGRÍAS

Alegrías I

Featured Techniques: rajeo, arpegio, and pulgar

109, 110

85

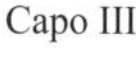

Capo III

♩ = 150 bpm

13
16
5/6CI
19
CI
22
25
CIII

Alegrías II

Featured Techniques: arpegio, ligado, picado, and rajeo

Capo III

♩ = 150 bpm

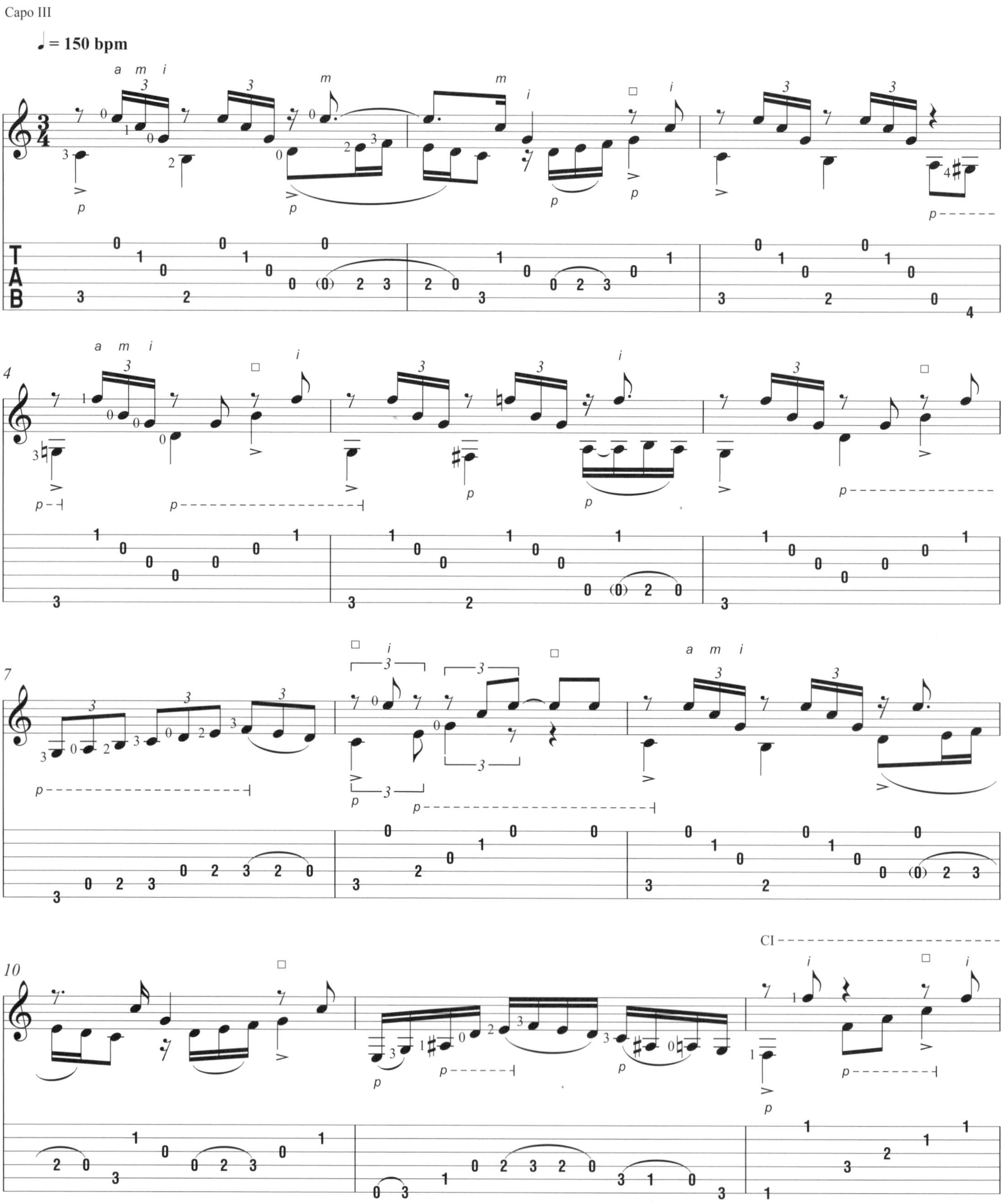

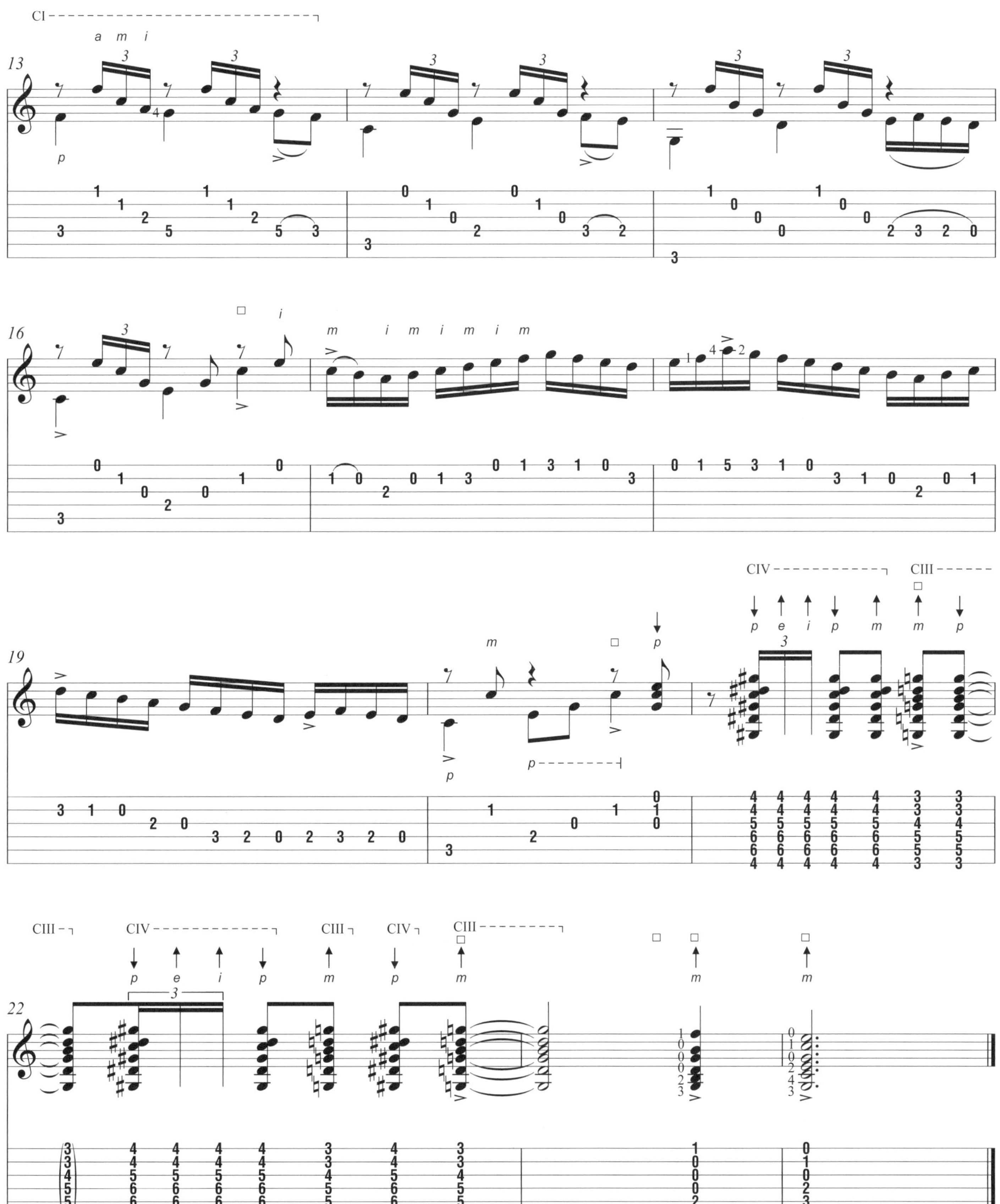

Alegrías III

Featured Techniques: pulgar, alzapúa, and arpegio

113, 114

87

Capo I

♩ = 150 bpm

13
16
19
22
25
CVII
5/6CVII

TANGOS

Tangos I

Featured Techniques: rajeo and arpegio

Capo III

♩ = 145 bpm

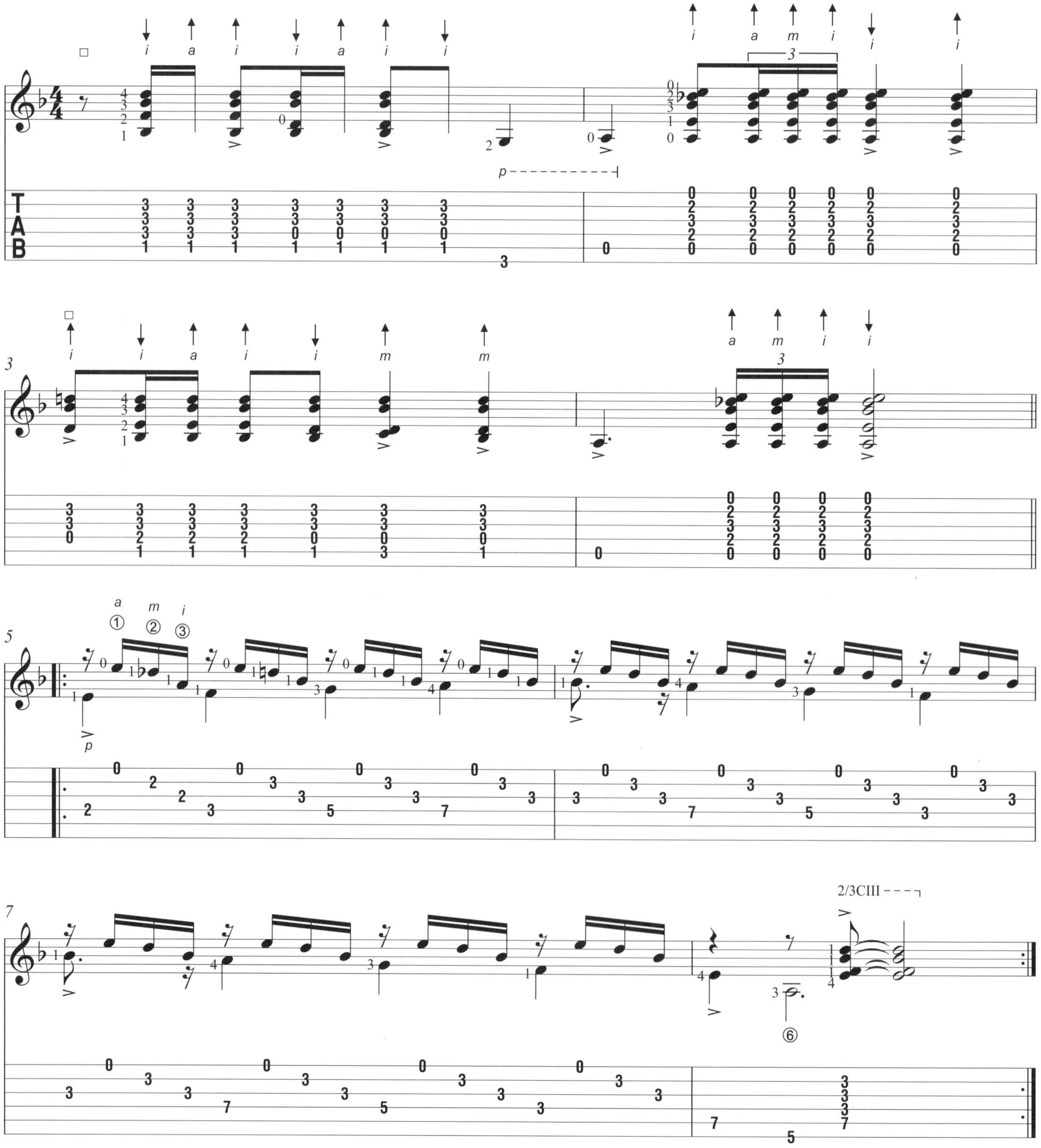

Tangos II

117, 118

89

This falseta in an arrangement of a popular melody of tangos de Granada.
Featured Techniques: picado, rajeo, and pulgar/índice

Capo III

♩ = 145 bpm

CI

Tangos: Rumba

Featured Techniques: arpegio, picado, and rajeo

119, 120

90

Capo III

♩ = 190 bpm

2/3CII

2/3CII
1.
14
2/3CII
2.
2/3CIV
2/3CII
2/3CI
17
2/3CI
2/3CII
2/3CIV
2/3CII
2/3CI
21

SOLEÁ POR BULERÍAS

Soleá por Bulerías I

Featured Techniques: arpegio, ligado, rajeo, and pulgar

Tuning, capo II:
(low to high) D-A-D-G-A-E

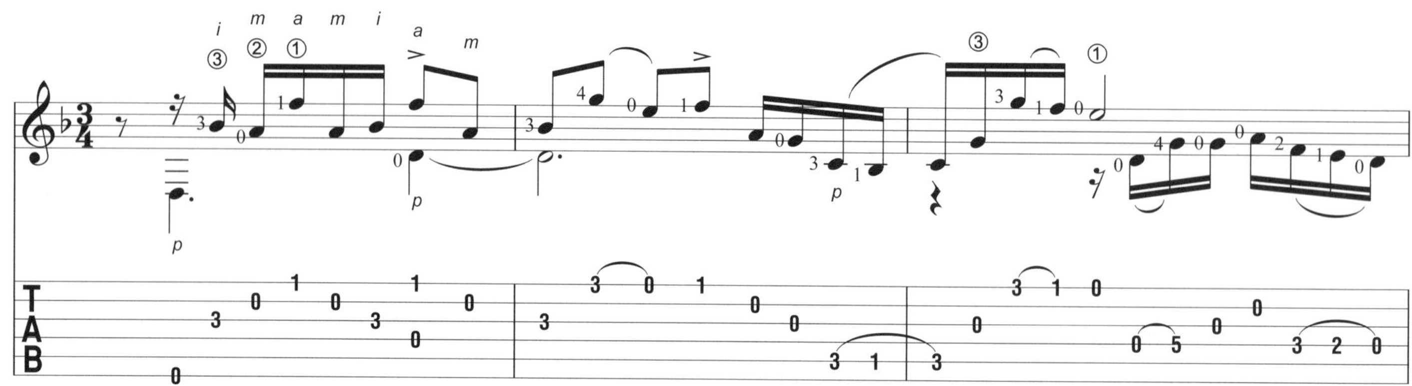

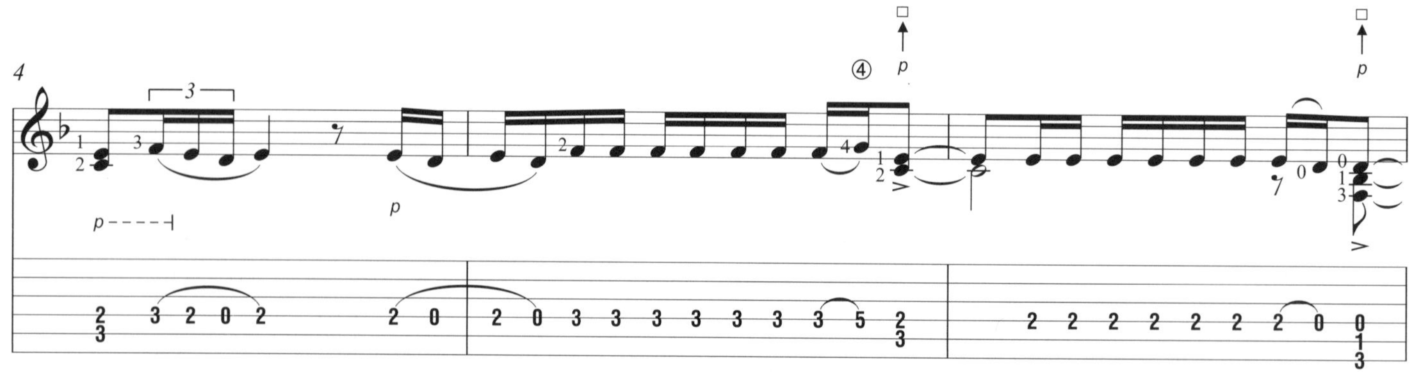

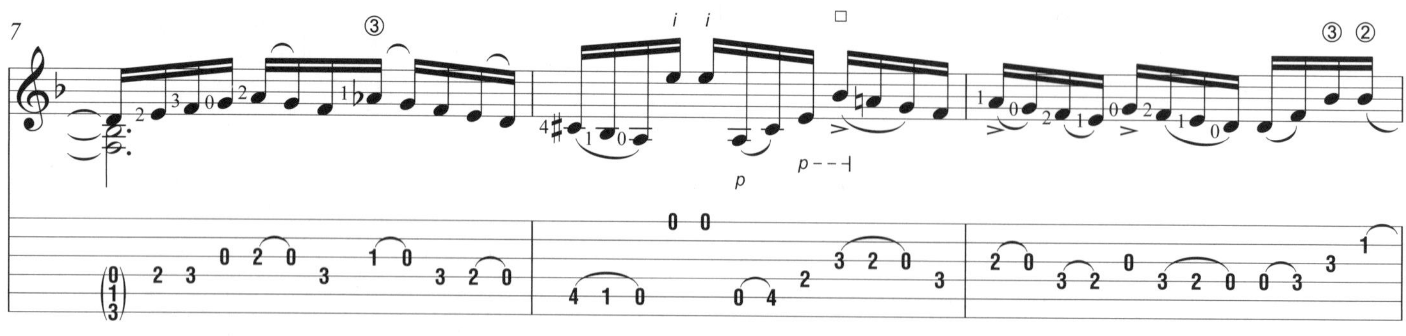

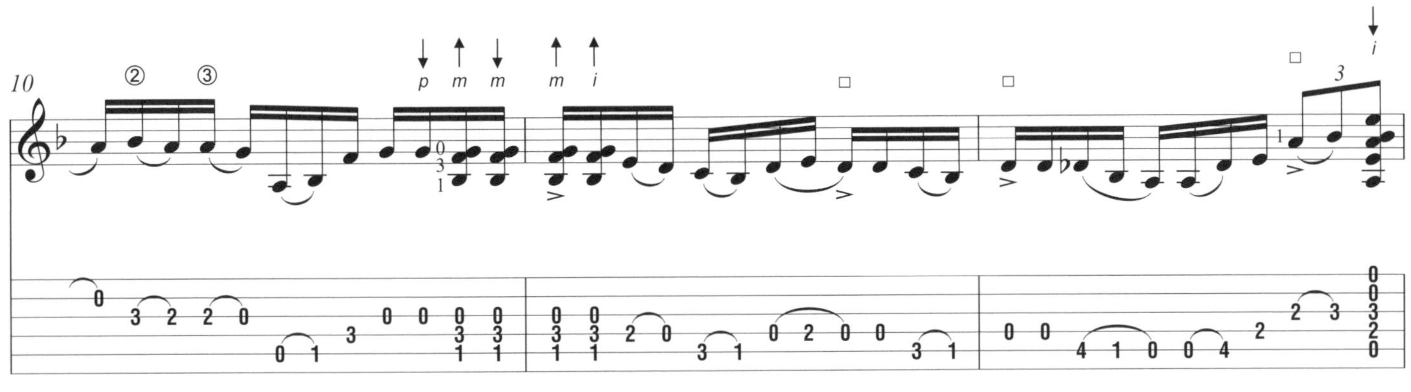

"Porcel" by José Porcel, 2017. Singers: David Vázquez, Pedro Obregón and Roberto Lorente; Percussion: Javier Fernández; Guitar: David Durán; Dancer: José Porcel. Photo by Beatrix Mexi Molnar.

Soleá por Bulerías II

Featured Techniques: pulgar and ligado

123, 124 92

Tuning, capo II:
(low to high) D-A-D-G-A-E

♩= 150 bpm

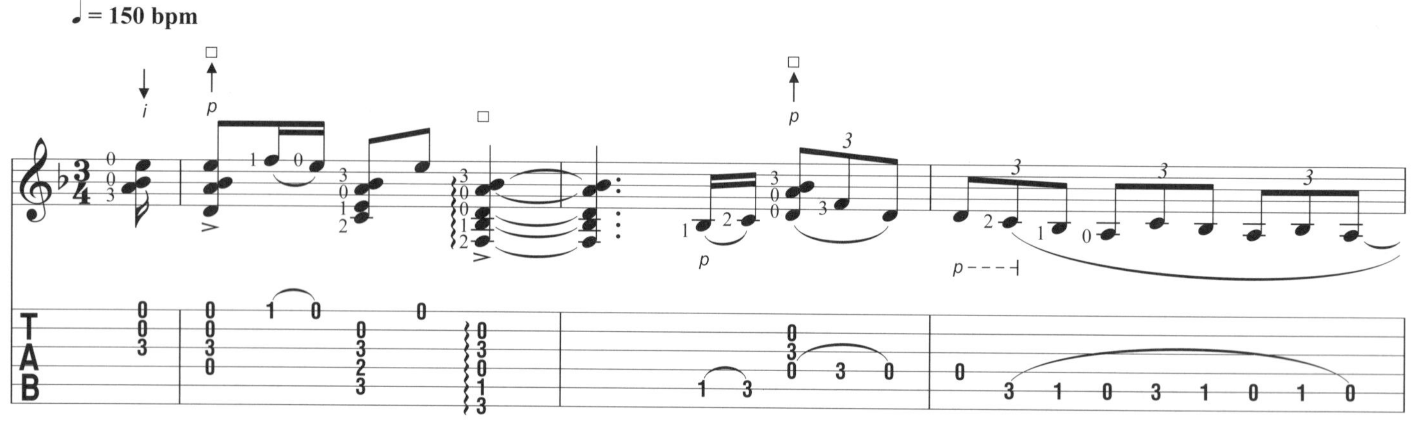

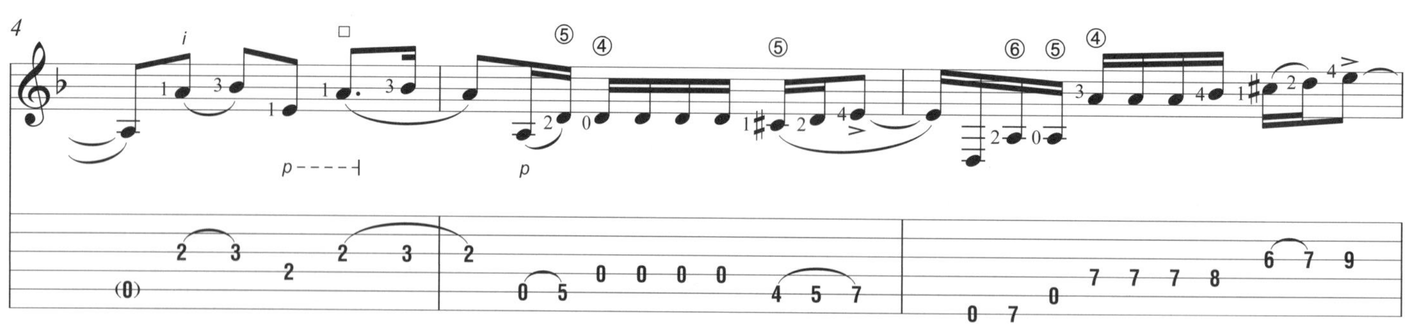

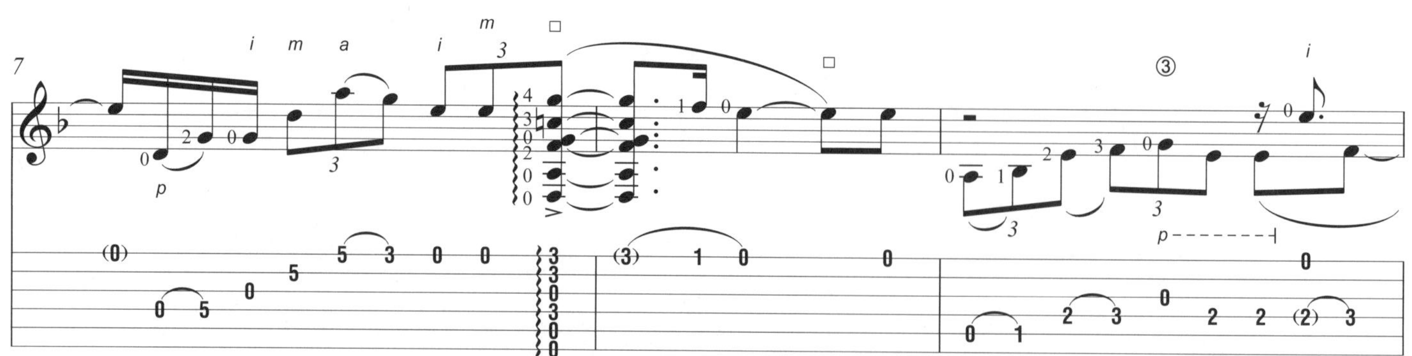

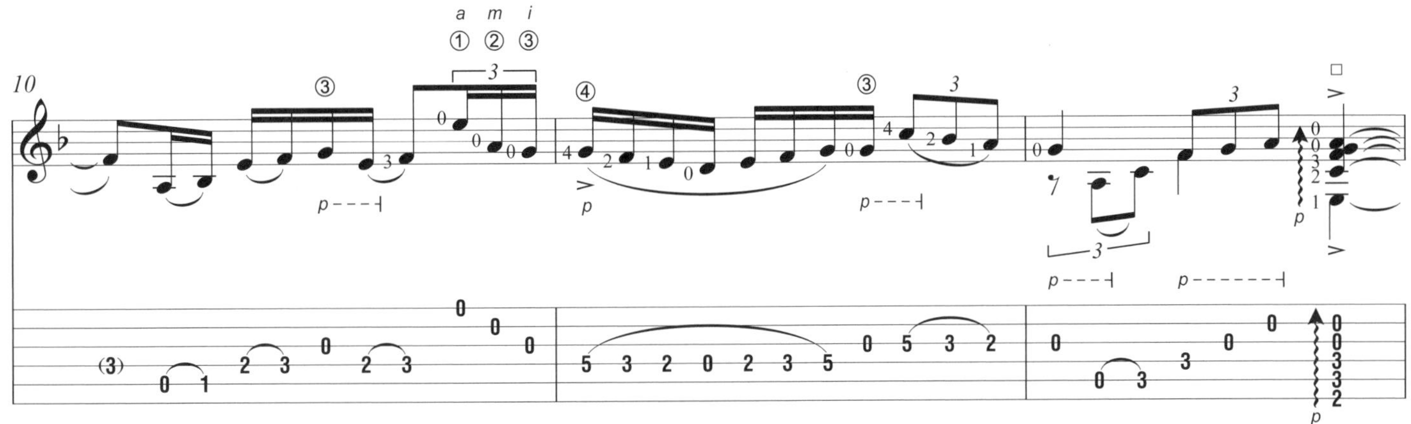
10
a m i
① ② ③
③
④
p
(3)

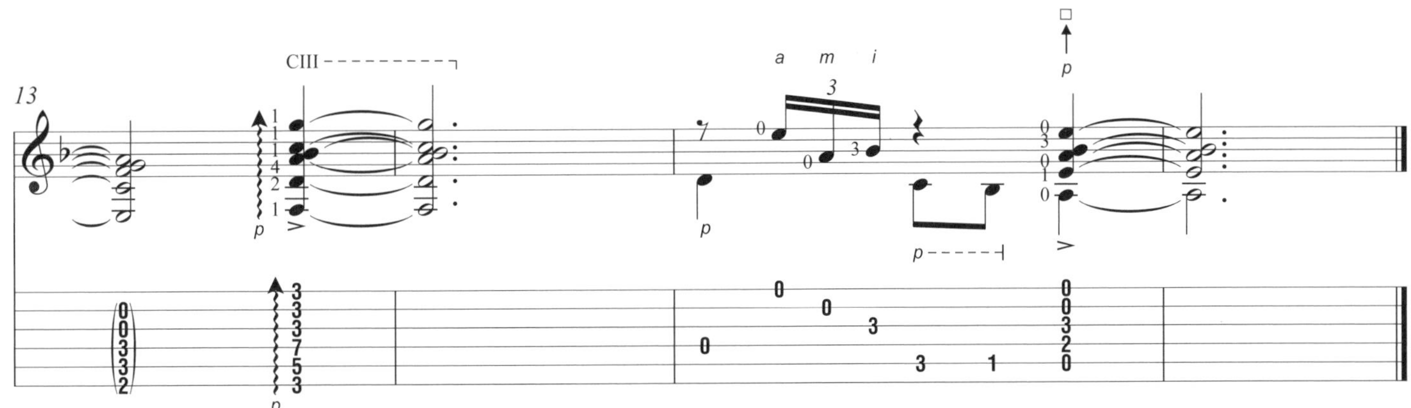
13
CIII
a m i
p

Soleá por Bulerías III

Featured Techniques: pulgar and ligado

125, 126

93

Tuning, capo II:
(low to high) D-A-D-G-A-E

♩= 150 bpm

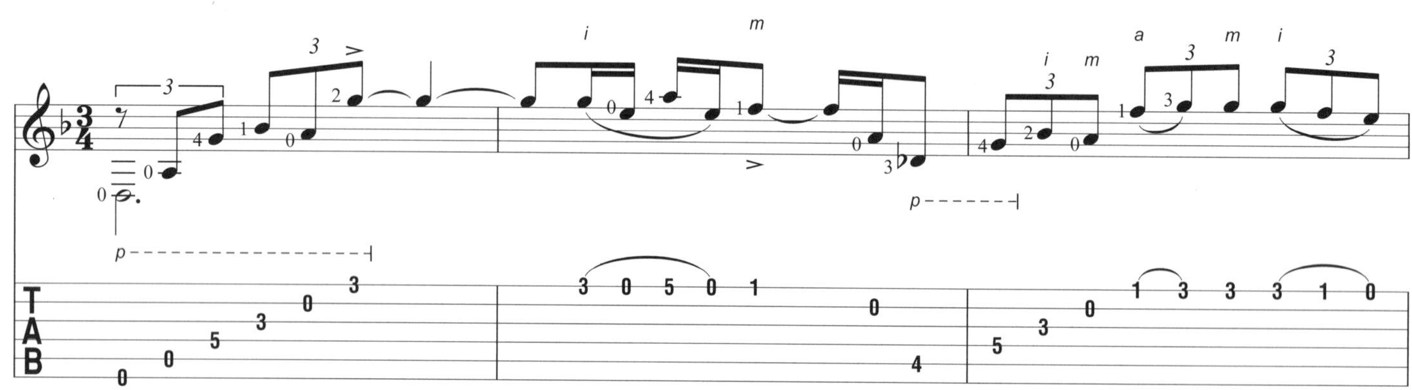

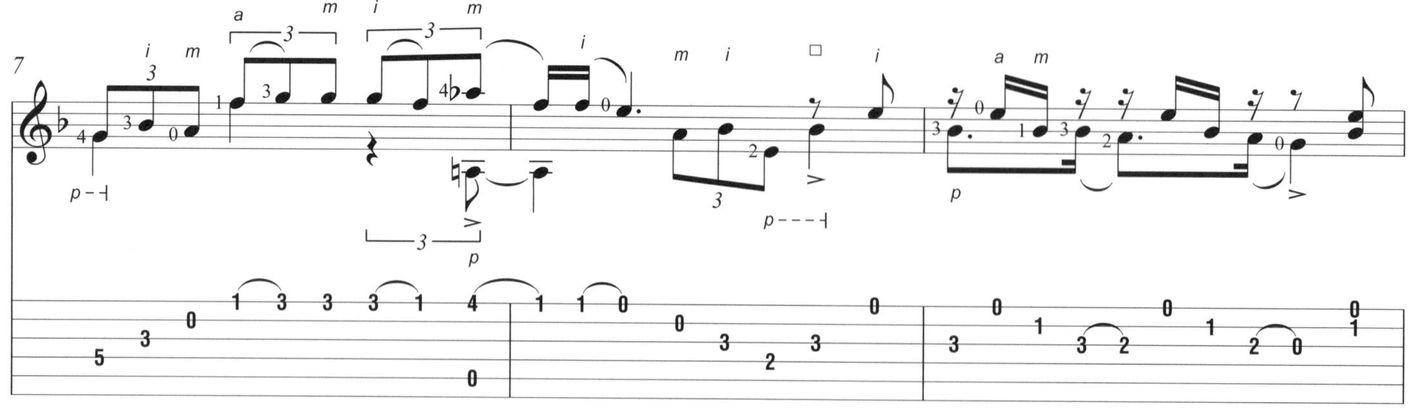

2/3CIII
2/3CII
p a m i

APPENDIX A

Recommended Listening

Manuel Agujetas, *El Rey del Cante Gitano*, Boa Music, feat Curro de Jeréz, CD10071, 1992.

Remedios Amaya, *Me Voy Contigo*, Hispavox, feat Vicente Amigo, José Luis Carmona, Tino di Geraldo, Carles Benavent and Chonchi Heredia, CD10119, 1997.

Vicente Amigo, *De Mi Corazón al Aire*, Sony Music, feat Javier Latorre, Antonio Carmona, Tino di Geraldo, Tito Duarte and Marcelo Fuentes, CD10157, 1991.

Vicente Amigo, *Vivencias Imaginadas*, Sony Music, feat Tino di Geraldo, Patricio Cámara, Duquende, Raquel Ramírez and Irapoan Freire, CD10155, 1995.

Various artists, *Canta Jerez*, Hispavox, feat Sordera, Fernando Terremoto, El Diamante Negro, El Borrico, Sernita and Romerito, CD22069, 1967.

Various artists, *V.OR.S. Jerez al Cante*, BBK, feat El Torta, Fernando de la Morena, Manuel Moneo, Luis "El Zambo," Manuel Agujetas and Capullo de Jerez, CD20360, 2012.

Various artists, *Antologia del Cante Flamenco*, Hispavox, feat Perico el del Lunar, Bernardo de los Lobitos, El Chaqueta, Niño de Almadén and Rafael Romero "El Gallina", CD20602, 1954.

Juan Manuel Cañizares, *Noches de Imán y Luna*, Nuevos Medios, CD15728, 1997.

Manolo Caracol, *Lo Mejor de Manolo Caracol*, Diamante, CD19448, 1979.

Moraíto Chico, *Morao Morao*, Discos Mercurio, feat Luis "El Zambo," La Venta, Maria Vala, Navajita Plateá, and Los Marismeños, CD15857, 1999, Reedited by Nuevos Medios in 2005.

Duquende, *Samaruco*, Universal Music Spain, feat Paco de Lucía and J.Manuel Cañizares, CD10655, 2006.

Fosforito, *Fosforito en los Cantes del Rincón de Cádiz*, Olivo, feat Enrique de Melchor, CD27016, 1979.

Manolo Franco, *Aljibe*, Pasarela S.L., CD19644, 1986.

Pepe Habichuela, *A Mandeli*, Nuevos Medios, CD10631, 1983.

Camarón de la Isla, *Potro de Rabia y Miel*, Phillips, feat Tomatito and Paco de Lucía, CD10484, 1991.

Carmen Linares, *Antología: La mujer en el cante*, Mercury, feat Vicente Amigo, Juan Habichuela, Tomatito, Rafael Riqueni, José Antonio Rodríguez, Moraíto, Enrique de Melchor, Manolo Franco, Miguel Ángel and Paco Cortés, CD10070, 1996.

Paco de Lucía, *Fuente y Caudal*, Universal Music Group, feat Ramón de Algeciras, CD13900, 1973.

Paco de Lucía, *Siroco*, Verve Records, feat Ramón de Algeciras, Pepe de Lucía, Jose María Bandera, Juan Ramírez and Rubén Dantas, CD10525, 1987.

Paco de Lucía, *Luzía*, Mercury, CD10527, 1998.

Juan Peña "El Lebrijano", *Persecucion*, Phillips, feat Pedro Peña and Enrique Marchena, CD20405, 1976.

La Macanita, *La Luna de Tomasa*, feat Diego del Morao and Moraíto Chico, CD22132, 2001.

Juan Talega, *Grands Cantaores du Flamenco Vol. 20*, Chante du Mond, CD10591.

Pepe Marchena, *Grands Cantaores du flamenco*, Chante du Mond, CD11816.

Antonio Mairena, *Grands Cantaores du flamenco*, Chante du Mond, CD10959.

Enrique Morente, *Morente sueña la Alhambra*, EMI, feat Estrella Morente, Tomatito, Alfredo Lagos, Carles Benavent and Pat Metheny, CD15237, 2006.

Estrella Morente, *Mi cante y un poema*, Virgin, feat Alfredo Lagos, Pepe Habichuela, Josemi Carmona, Juan Habichuela, Manolo Sanlúcar and Montoyita, CD12470, 2001.

Gerardo Nuñez, *Andando el Tiempo*, ACT, feat Carmén Cortés, Cepillo, Perico Sambeat, Paolo Fresu and Pablo Martín Caminero, CD14632, 2004.

Enrique de Melchor, *La noche y el día*, Fonomusic, feat José Mercé, Vicente Soto "Sordera," Jose Menese, Juan Parrilla and Antonio Carmona CD22244, 1991.

Niño Miguel, *Diferente*, Universal Music Group, CD15905, 1976.

Victor Monge "Serranito," *Guitarra Flamenca*, Hispavox, CD22689, 1971.

Ramón Montoya, *Grandes Figures du Flamenco VOL.5*, Le Chante du Mond, CD9402, 1988.

Diego del Morao, *Orate*, Cigala Music, feat Diego el Cigala, Niña Pastori, Paco de Lucía, Diego Carrasco, Juan Carrasco and Moraíto Chico, CD19712, 2010.

El Pele, *Canto*, BMG Spain, feat Vicente Amigo, CD50511, 2003.

Niño Ricardo, *Grandes Figures du Flamenco*, Harmonia Mundi, CD9397, 1991.

Rafael Riqueni, *Mi Tiempo*, Nuevos Medios, feat Antonio Canales, Antonio Carmona and Antonio Reyes, CD 10792, 1990.

Juan Carlos Romero, *Agua Encendida*, Nuba Records, feat José Mercé, José Valencia, La Susi, Los Mellis, Mercedes Amador and Mamá Carmen, CD19676, 2010.

Sabicas, *El Rey del Flamenco*, ABC Records, CD10289, 1965.

Manolo Sanlúcar, *Tauromagia*, Polygram, feat Diego Carrasco, José Mercé, La Macanita, EL Moro, Isidro Sanlúcar and Tino di Geraldo, CD10145, 1988.

Tomatito, *Guitarra Gitana*, Nuevos Medios, feat Jorge Pardo, Raimundo Amador, Paquete, Juan Carmona, Remedios Amaya, Potito, Chonchi and Dieguito, CD10153, 1996.

El Viejín, *Algo que Decir*, Nuevos Medios, feat Paco de Lucía, Carles Benavent, Monse Cortés, Antonio Canales and Juan Ramírez, CD15749, 1999.

APPENDIX B

Alternative Tunings

In flamenco guitar, besides the standard tuning of the guitar, it is common to find alternative tunings ("scordaturas") in order to create more expressive and profound sonorities—fresh sounds that make the traditional cadences sound new and updated.

The first scordatura that appeared in flamenco guitar is the D tuning: the sixth string is lowered by one whole step, so now, the instrument has two open strings in D (fourth and sixth).

Standard Tuning

D Tuning

FIG. B.1. Standard Tuning vs. D Tuning

We can find this tuning in the flamenco guitar method of Rafael Marín (1902) and later in the early guajiras of Ramón Montoya and the "Zapateado in D" of Sabicas. This tuning was first used to play in D Ionian/Aeolian with an open D chord in first position. Then, we see it used for playing in A Phrygian (por medio) with a modal character, as we see in the "Seguiriyas in D" by Sabicas. Other masterpieces that use this tuning include:

Classic Recordings Using D Tuning		
Song	**Palo**	**Artist**
"Farruca de Lucía"	Farruca	Paco de Lucía
"Monaterio de Sal"	Colombiana	Paco de Lucía
"Cagancho"	Seguiriya	Rafael Riqueni

However, the most famous and functional alternative tuning is the one used in rondeña, which became popular when the master Ramón Montoya recorded it, first in 1923 and later in 1936. In this case, he lowered the sixth string a whole step below and the third string a half step below: D A D F♯ B E. The unique key used with this tuning is C♯ Phrygian.

Standard Tuning

Rondeña
(Ramón Montoya)

FIG. B.2. Standard Tuning vs. Rondeña Tuning

This innovative tuning has been used in many other palos, and in vocal accompaniment since 1972, when Paco de Lucía recorded the famous "Canastera" with Camarón de la Isla. Other masterpieces that contain this tuning are below.

Classic Recordings Using Rodeña Tuning		
Song	**Palo**	**Artist**
"Recuerdos"	Bulerías	Niño Miguel
"Gañanía"	Soleá por Bulerías	Diego del Morao
"Sierra del Agua"	Rondeña	Vicente Amigo

Another interesting alternative tuning is the one used by Esteban de Sanlúcar in his famous composition, *Mantilla de Feria*. An open G tuning (borrowed from classical guitar) was introduced by tuning the guitar to D, G, D, G, B, E (from bass to treble).

Standard Tuning

G Tuning

FIG. B.3. Standard Tuning vs. G Tuning

This tuning, being primarily limited to G major, can be found in these recordings.

Classic Recordings Using G Tuning		
Song	**Palo**	**Artist**
"Danza mora"	Arabian Dance	Sabicas
"De la vera"	Garrotín	Rafael Riqueni

Since the 1980s, there has been a real fever among flamenco guitarist to seek new tunings, especially during the early nineties. These new tunings gave a more dissonant sound to flamenco, by facilitating the use of different open strings, and led to the development of the contemporary flamenco guitar style. Here are some examples.

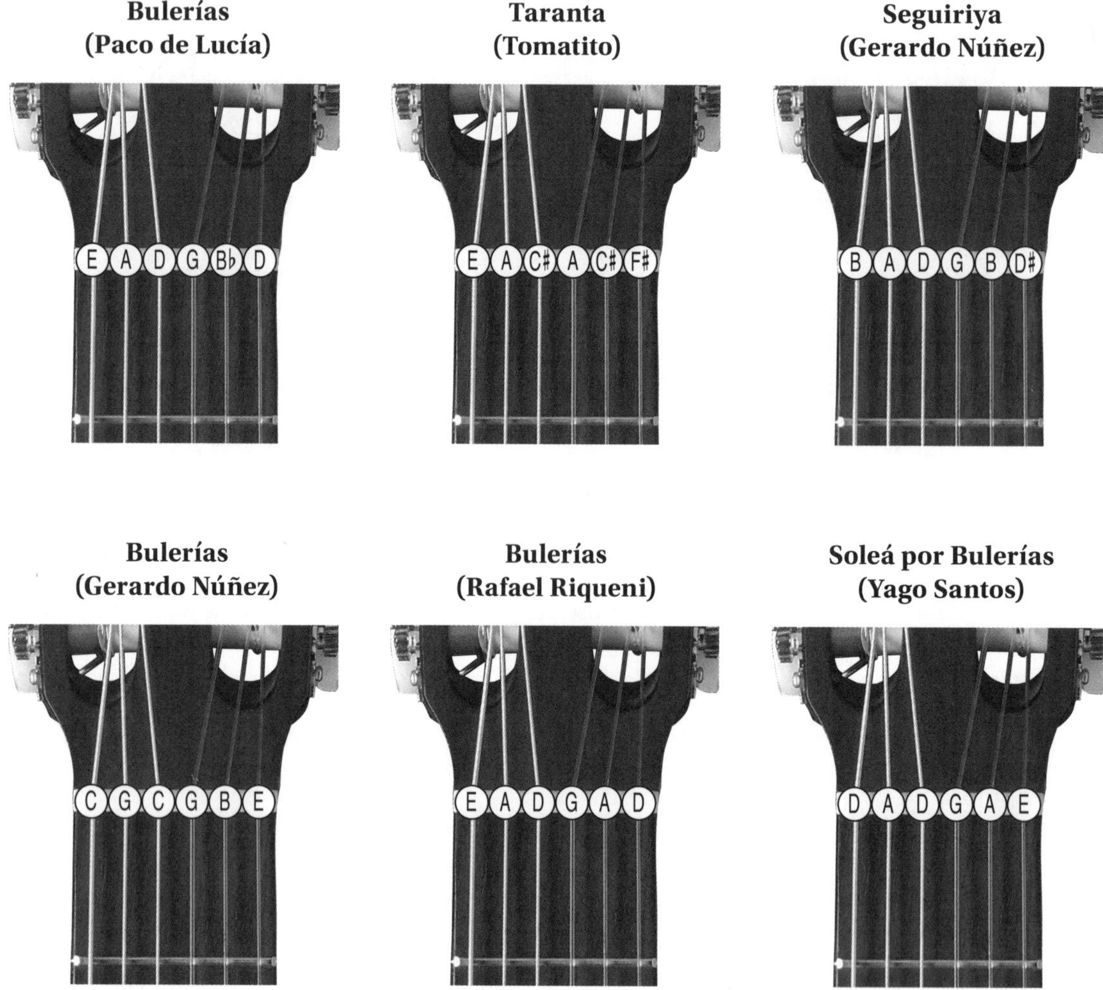

FIG. B.4. Alternative Tunings in Contemporary Flamenco

APPENDIX C

Glossary of Spanish Guitar Terms

abanico (a.βa.'ni.ko)	literally "fan." Refers to a subcategory of *rasgueo*, using either *p, e, i* and *p, m*. Alternative methods include *p, ma* or *p, a, i*.
acento (a.'sε̃n̪.to)	accent
a compás (a kõm.'pas)	on rhythm
acorde (a.'koɾ.ðe)	chord
aficionado (a.fi.sjo.'na.ðo)	someone that is interested in flamenco music.
afinador (a.fi.na.'ðoɾ)	tuner. From Spanish "afinar" meaning "to tune."
al aire (al 'ai̯.ɾe)	open (string)
alzapúa (al.sa.'pwa)	using the thumb (*p*) to articulate a combination of single notes and parts of chords.
anular (a.nu.'laɾ)	ring finger (notated as "*a*")
a palo seco (a.'ðoɾ.no)	group of *palos* performed without guitar accompaniment.
apoyando (a.po.'ɟã n̪.do)	from Spanish "apoyar" meaning "support." Strings are struck towards the soundboard in such way that the striking finger is caught and supported by the next string.
aros ('a.ɾos)	sides of the guitar
arpegio (aɾ.'pe.xjo)	plucking individual notes of a chord, e.g., *p, i, m, a, m, i*
arrastre (a.'ras.tɾe)	glissé or slide
arreglo (a.'re.ɣlo)	arrangement
bailaor (bai̯.la.'oɾ)	male flamenco dancer
bailaora (bai̯.la.'o.ɾa)	female flamenco dancer
baile ('bai̯.le)	flamenco dance
bajo ('ba.xo)	bass
bemol (be.'mol)	flat

blanca ('blaŋ.ka)	literally "white." Cypress-made flamenco guitar.
boca ('bo.ka)	sound hole of the guitar
bordones (boɾ.'ðo.nes)	three lowest strings of the guitar (4, 5, 6)
cabeza (ka.'βe.sa)	head of the flamenco guitar
cadencia (ka.'ðɛ̃n.sja)	cadence
caja ('ka.xa)	sound box of the guitar
cajón (ka.'xõn)	percussion instrument, originally from Perú similar to an empty wooden box. Introduced to flamenco music by Paco de Lucía during one of his tours on that country.
cantaor (kãn̪.ta.'oɾ)	male flamenco singer
cantaora (kãn̪.ta.'o.ɾa)	female flamenco singer
cante ('kãn̪.te)	flamenco singing
cejilla (se.'xi.ɟa)	barré, the stopping of all or several strings at the same fret by the index finger of the fretboard hand/capo.
chasqueo (ʧas.'ke.o)	buzzing
cierre ('sjɛ.re)	last measure of a remate
clavijero (kla.βi.'xɛ.ɾo)	tuning peg
coletilla (ko.lɛ.'ti.ɟa)	tag, short refrain at the end of a flamenco stanza
compás (kõm.'pas)	beat, rhythm, measure
copla ('kop̚.la)	literally "couplet." A type of stanza or estrofa used in flamenco literature. Each copla is usually three or four verses (*tercios*) long, of octosyllabic lines.
cromática (kɾo.'ma.ti.ka)	chromatic
cuadro ('kwa.ðɾo)	literally "painting." Flamenco musicians use this word to refer to a group of flamenco performers, including the dancer, singer and guitar player.
cuerda ('kwɛɾ.ða)	string
derecha (dɛ.'re.ʧa)	right hand (i.e., strumming hand)
detalle (dɛ.'ta.ɟe)	literally "detail," much shorter than a falseta, generally one or half measure long.
diapasón (dja.pa.'sõn)	fingerboard of the guitar
digitación (di.xi.ta.'sjõn)	fingering
ejercicio (e.xɛɾ.'si.sjo)	exercise
escala (ɛs.'ka.la)	scale
escobilla (ɛs.ko.'βi.ɟa)	literally "broom." Concrete inner-structure passages of certain palos/bailes, such as soleá or alegrías.
estrofa (ɛs.tro.fa)	strophe, a section of a lyric
falseta (fal.'sɛ.ta)	a prepared or improvised guitar-focused variation.

fondo ('fõn̪.do)	back of the guitar
golpe ('gol.pe)	literally "hit." Tap on the sound box.
golpeador (gol.pe.a.'ðoɾ)	tapping plate
guitarra (gi.'ta.ra)	guitar
guitarrero (gi.ta.'rɛ.ɾo)	guitar builder
hacia abajo ('a.sja a.'βa.xo)	downward
hacia arriba ('a.sja a.'ri.βa)	upward
hueso ('we.so)	saddle of the guitar
índice ('ĩn̪.di.se)	index finger (notated as "*i*")
izquierda (is.'kjɛɾ.ða)	left hand (i.e., fretboard hand)
jaleo (xa.'le.o)	shouts of encouragement to cheer the performers in a flamenco show ("olé" or "vamos allá" are the most frequent *jaleos*).
letras ('lɛ.tɾas)	lyrics/words
ligado (li.'ɣa.ðo)	slur
llamada (ɟʝa.'ma.ða)	literally "call." Specific set of footwork that lets the dancer communicate with the singer and the guitar player that a change or an ending is coming.
mano ('ma.no)	hand
mástil ('mas.til)	fretboard
mayor (ma.'ʝoɾ)	major (key)
media cejilla ('me.ðja se.'xi.ʝa)	semi-barré
medio ('me.ðjo)	middle finger (notated as "*m*")
menor (me.'noɾ)	minor (key)
meñique (me.'ɲi.ke)	little finger (notated "*e*")
negra ('ne.ɣɾa)	literally "black." Rosewood-made flamenco guitar.
nudillos (nu.'ði.ʝos)	knuckles
palmas ('pal.mas)	rhythmic hand claps that accompany a performance.
palo ('pa.lo)	flamenco song/form (e.g., *solea, tangos, bulerias, alegrias,* etc.)
pellizco (pe.'ʝis.ko)	literally "nip, pinch." An artist's or performance's distinctive sense of infectious rhythm.
picado (pi.'ka.ðo)	playing single note melodies using *i, m* or *m, i.* Alternative methods include *i, a* and *m, a.*
pié ('pje)	foot
por arriba (poɾ a.'ri.βa)	E Phrygian tonality
por medio (poɾ 'me.ðjo)	A Phrygian tonality

posición (po.si.'sjõn) — the position or setting of the fingers of the fretting hand for playing of a chord, arpegio, or passage.

posturas (pos.'tu.ɾas) — flamenco guitarist term for "chords"

primas ('priːməz) — first three strings of the guitar

puente ('pwɛ̃n̪.te) — bridge of the flamenco guitar

pulgar (pul.'ɣaɾ) — thumb (notated as "*p*")

pulgar/índice (pul.'ɣaɾ 'ĩn̪.di.se) — thumb/index

pulsación (pul.sa.'sjõn) — the action or "feel" of the guitar strings; in flamenco music, it also refers to the rhythmic feel and sound of a guitar player.

rajeo (ra.xe.o) — (also *rasgueo* or *rasgueado*) the strumming of chords peculiar to the flamenco guitar in ascending or descending order of notes.

remate (re.'ma.te) — last couple of measures of a falseta or of a particular *baile* or *cante*.

soniquete (so.ni.'kɛ.te) — literally "droning." Flamenco rhythm mastery.

sostenido (sos.te.'ni.ðo) — sharp

tablao (ta.'βla.o) — bar or club with stage for flamenco shows

tapa ('ta.pa) — top of the flamenco guitar

templar (tɛ̃m.'plaɾ) — to tune

tercio ('tɛɾ.sjo) — literally "thirds." Each single verses or musical phrases of a flamenco song.

tiempos ('tjɛ̃m.pos) — beats

tirando (ti.'ɾãn̪.do) — free or unsupported plucking strokes

tocaor (to.ka.'oɾ) — flamenco guitarist

tocar (to.'kaɾ) — to play

tono ('to.no) — "pitch" or "key"

toque ('to.ke) — the art of flamenco guitar playing

toque gitano ('to.ke xi.'ta.no) — gypsy style of guitar playing

trastes ('tɾas.tes) — frets of the guitar

trémolo ('tɾe.mo.lo) — strumming hand technique that consists on playing one bass note and three upper notes with the following fingering: *p*, *i*, *a*, *m*, *i*

zapateado (sa.pa.te.'a.ðo) — footwork/dance steps

ABOUT THE AUTHOR

Born December 28, 1985 and raised in Bilbao (Spain), Yago Santos is a student of the master Rafael Riqueni. He has toured internationally as a soloist and also shared the stage with flamenco artists such as José Mercé, Manuel Molina, Rafael Riqueni, El Pele, José el de la Tomasa, and Mayte Martín. Yago holds a master's degree from Berklee College of Music, where he received a full scholarship and graduated summa cum laude. Two months after graduating from Berklee, he won the first International Paco de Lucía Prize at the International Guitar Competition of Seville and collaborated with Hans Zimmer and Lorne Balfe on the EMI nominated series *Genius: Picasso* (National Geographic). His first solo album was released in 2020.

These two tracks are from his solo album, *Alma de Niño* (2020).

5, 93

More Guitar Publications

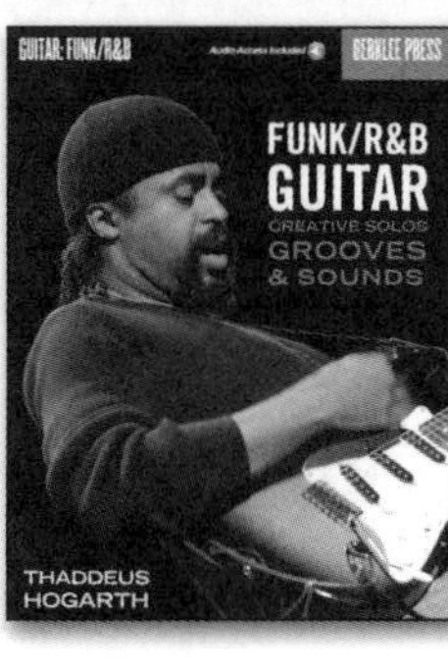

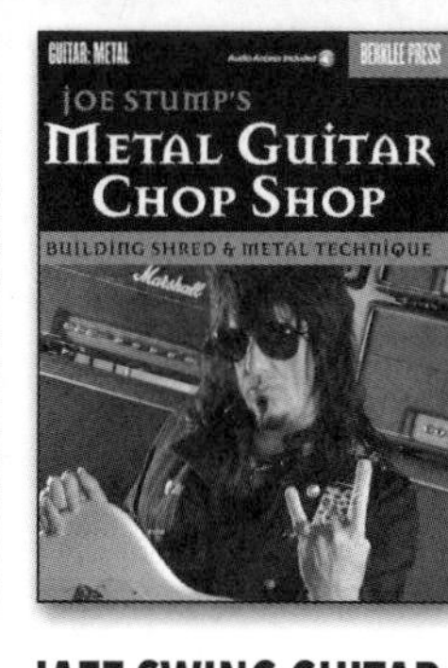

ADVANCED READING STUDIES FOR GUITAR
William Leavitt
50449500 Book $19.99

BEBOP GUITAR SOLOS
Michael Kaplan
00121703 Book $16.99

BERKLEE BASIC GUITAR
William Leavitt
50449460 Phase 1 Book $12.99
50449470 Phase 2 Book $14.99

BERKLEE BLUES GUITAR SONGBOOK
Michael Williams
50449593 Book/Online Audio $27.99

BERKLEE ESSENTIAL GUITAR SONGBOOK
Kim Perlak, Sheryl Bailey, and Members of the Berklee Guitar Department Faculty
00350814 Book $19.99

BERKLEE GUITAR CHORD DICTIONARY
Rick Peckham
50449546 Book - Jazz $14.99
50449596 Book - Rock $12.99

BERKLEE GUITAR STYLE STUDIES
Jim Kelly
00200377 Book/Online Media $24.99

BERKLEE GUITAR THEORY
Kim Perlak and Members of the Berklee Guitar Department Faculty
00276326 Book $24.99

BERKLEE JAZZ STANDARDS FOR SOLO GUITAR
John Stein
50449653 Book/Online Audio $22.99

BERKLEE PRACTICE METHOD FOR GUITAR
Larry Baione
50449426 Book/CD $19.99

BERKLEE SOLO UKULELE
Karen Hogg
00327666 Book/Online Audio $16.99

BLUES GUITAR TECHNIQUE
Michael Williams
50449623 Book/Online Audio $29.99

THE CHORD FACTORY
Jon Damian
50449541 Book $27.99

Visit your local music dealer or bookstore,
or go to **www.berkleepress.com**
Prices and availability subject to change without notice

CLASSICAL STUDIES FOR PICK-STYLE GUITAR
William Leavitt
50449440 Book $14.99

CLASSICAL TECHNIQUE FOR THE MODERN GUITARIST
Kim Perlak
00148781 Book/Online Audio $19.99

CONTEMPORARY JAZZ GUITAR SOLOS
Michael Kaplan
00143596 Book $16.99

COUNTRY GUITAR STYLES
Mike Ihde
00254157 Book/Online Audio $24.99

CREATIVE CHORDAL HARMONY FOR GUITAR
Mick Goodrick and Tim Miller
50449613 Book/Online Audio $22.99

FUNK/R&B GUITAR
Thaddeus Hogarth
50449569 Book/Online Audio $19.99

GUITAR SWEEP PICKING & ARPEGGIOS
Joe Stump
00151223 Book/Online Audio $19.99

THE GUITARIST'S GUIDE TO COMPOSING AND IMPROVISING
Jon Damian
50449497 Book/Online Audio $24.99

INTRODUCTION TO JAZZ GUITAR
Jane Miller
00125041 Book/Online Audio $22.99

JAZZ GUITAR FRETBOARD NAVIGATION
Mark White
00154107 Book/Online Audio $22.99

JAZZ GUITAR IMPROVISATION STRATEGIES
Steven Kirby
00274977 Book/Online Media $26.99

JAZZ IMPROVISATION FOR GUITAR
Garrison Fewell
50449594 Book/Online Audio - Harmonic Approach .. $29.99
50449503 Book/Online Audio - Melodic Approach..... $27.99

Berklee Press

JAZZ SWING GUITAR
Jon Wheatley
00139935 Book/Online Audio $24.99

MELODIC RHYTHMS FOR GUITAR
William Leavitt
50449450 Book $17.99

Joe Stump's
METAL GUITAR CHOP SHOP
50449601 Book/Online Audio $19.99

MODAL VOICING TECHNIQUES FOR GUITAR
Rick Peckham
00151227 Book/Online Video $24.99

A MODERN METHOD FOR GUITAR
William Leavitt
50449400 Volume 1 Book $15.99
50449404 Volume 1 Book/Online Audio $24.99
00137387 Volume 1 Book/Online Video $24.99
50449410 Volume 2 Book $16.99
50448021 Volume 2 Book/Online Audio $24.99
50449420 Volume 3 Book $19.99
00292989 Volume 3 Book/Online Audio $24.99
50449468 Volumes 1-3 Book $39.99
00292990 Volumes 1-3 Book/Online Media $49.99

A MODERN METHOD FOR GUITAR SCALES
Larry Baione
00199318 Book $14.99

A MODERN METHOD FOR GUITAR SONGBOOKS
50449539 Jazz with Online Audio $22.99
50449624 Rock with CD $17.99

PLAYING THE CHANGES: GUITAR
Mitch Seidman and Paul Del Nero
50449509 Book/CD $24.99

THE PRACTICAL JAZZ GUITARIST
Mark White
50449618 Book/Online Audio $27.99

THE PRIVATE GUITAR STUDIO HANDBOOK
Mike McAdam
00121641 Book $14.99

READING STUDIES FOR GUITAR
William Leavitt
50449490 Book $17.99

TRIADS FOR THE IMPROVISING GUITARIST
Jane Miller
00284857 Book/Online Audio $22.99

More Fine Publications

GUITAR

BEBOP GUITAR SOLOS
by Michael Kaplan
00121703 Book.......$16.99

BLUES GUITAR TECHNIQUE
by Michael Williams
50449623 Book/Online Audio.......$27.99

BERKLEE GUITAR CHORD DICTIONARY
by Rick Peckham
50449546 Jazz - Book.......$14.99
50449596 Rock - Book.......$12.99

BERKLEE GUITAR STYLE STUDIES
by Jim Kelly
00200377 Book/Online Media.......$24.99

CLASSICAL TECHNIQUE FOR THE MODERN GUITARIST
by Kim Perlak
00148781 Book/Online Audio.......$19.99

CONTEMPORARY JAZZ GUITAR SOLOS
by Michael Kaplan
00143596 Book.......$16.99

CREATIVE CHORDAL HARMONY FOR GUITAR
by Mick Goodrick and Tim Miller
50449613 Book/Online Audio.......$22.99

FUNK/R&B GUITAR
by Thaddeus Hogarth
50449569 Book/Online Audio.......$19.99

GUITAR SWEEP PICKING
by Joe Stump
00151223 Book/Online Audio.......$19.99

INTRODUCTION TO JAZZ GUITAR
by Jane Miller
00125041 Book/Online Audio.......$22.99

JAZZ GUITAR FRETBOARD NAVIGATION
by Mark White
00154107 Book/Online Audio.......$22.99

JAZZ SWING GUITAR
by Jon Wheatley
00139935 Book/Online Audio.......$24.99

METAL GUITAR CHOP SHOP
by Joe Stump
50449601 Book/Online Audio.......$19.99

A MODERN METHOD FOR GUITAR – VOLUMES 1-3 COMPLETE*
by William Leavitt
00292990 Book/Online Media.......$49.99
**Individual volumes, media options, and supporting songbooks available.*

A MODERN METHOD FOR GUITAR SCALES
by Larry Baione
00199318 Book.......$14.99

READING STUDIES FOR GUITAR
by William Leavitt
50449490 Book.......$17.99

Berklee Press publications feature material developed at Berklee College of Music.
To browse the complete Berklee Press Catalog, go to
www.berkleepress.com

BASS

BERKLEE JAZZ BASS
by Rich Appleman, Whit Browne & Bruce Gertz
50449636 Book/Online Audio.......$22.99

CHORD STUDIES FOR ELECTRIC BASS
by Rich Appleman & Joseph Viola
50449750 Book.......$17.99

FINGERSTYLE FUNK BASS LINES
by Joe Santerre
50449542 Book/Online Audio.......$19.99

FUNK BASS FILLS
by Anthony Vitti
50449608 Book/Online Audio.......$22.99

INSTANT BASS
by Danny Morris
50449502 Book/CD.......$9.99

METAL BASS LINES
by David Marvuglio
00122465 Book/Online Audio.......$19.99

READING CONTEMPORARY ELECTRIC BASS
by Rich Appleman
50449770 Book.......$22.99

ROCK BASS LINES
by Joe Santerre
50449478 Book/Online Audio.......$22.99

PIANO/KEYBOARD

BERKLEE JAZZ KEYBOARD HARMONY
by Suzanna Sifter
00138874 Book/Online Audio.......$29.99

BERKLEE JAZZ PIANO
by Ray Santisi
50448047 Book/Online Audio.......$22.99

BERKLEE JAZZ STANDARDS FOR SOLO PIANO
arr. Robert Christopherson, Hey Rim Jeon, Ross Ramsay, Tim Ray
00160482 Book/Online Audio.......$19.99

CHORD-SCALE IMPROVISATION FOR KEYBOARD
by Ross Ramsay
50449597 Book/CD.......$19.99

CONTEMPORARY PIANO TECHNIQUE
by Stephany Tiernan
50449545 Book/DVD.......$29.99

HAMMOND ORGAN COMPLETE
by Dave Limina
00237801 Book/Online Audio.......$24.99

JAZZ PIANO COMPING
by Suzanne Davis
50449614 Book/Online Audio.......$22.99

LATIN JAZZ PIANO IMPROVISATION
by Rebecca Cline
50449649 Book/Online Audio.......$29.99

PIANO ESSENTIALS
by Ross Ramsay
50448046 Book/Online Audio.......$24.99

SOLO JAZZ PIANO
by Neil Olmstead
50449641 Book/Online Audio.......$42.99

DRUMS

BEGINNING DJEMBE
by Michael Markus & Joe Galeota
00148210 Book/Online Video.......$16.99

BERKLEE JAZZ DRUMS
by Casey Scheuerell
50449612 Book/Online Audio.......$24.99

DRUM SET WARM-UPS
by Rod Morgenstein
50449465 Book.......$14.99

A MANUAL FOR THE MODERN DRUMMER
by Alan Dawson & Don DeMichael
50449560 Book.......$14.99

MASTERING THE ART OF BRUSHES
by Jon Hazilla
50449459 Book/Online Audio.......$19.99

PHRASING
by Russ Gold
00120209 Book/Online Media.......$19.99

WORLD JAZZ DRUMMING
by Mark Walker
50449568 Book/CD.......$22.99

BERKLEE PRACTICE METHOD

GET YOUR BAND TOGETHER
With additional volumes for other instruments, plus a teacher's guide.

Bass
by Rich Appleman, John Repucci and the Berklee Faculty
50449427 Book/CD.......$24.99

Drum Set
by Ron Savage, Casey Scheuerell and the Berklee Faculty
50449429 Book/CD.......$17.99

Guitar
by Larry Baione and the Berklee Faculty
50449426 Book/CD.......$19.99

Keyboard
by Russell Hoffmann, Paul Schmeling and the Berklee Faculty
50449428 Book/Online Audio.......$19.99

VOICE

BELTING
by Jeannie Gagné
00124984 Book/Online Media.......$22.99

THE CONTEMPORARY SINGER
by Anne Peckham
50449595 Book/Online Audio.......$27.99

JAZZ VOCAL IMPROVISATION
by Mili Bermejo
00159290 Book/Online Audio.......$19.99

TIPS FOR SINGERS
by Carolyn Wilkins
50449557 Book/CD.......$19.95

VOCAL WORKOUTS FOR THE CONTEMPORARY SINGER
by Anne Peckham
50448044 Book/Online Audio.......$24.99

YOUR SINGING VOICE
by Jeannie Gagné
50449619 Book/Online Audio.......$29.99